Leading *with* BILLY GRAHAM

The Leadership Principles and Life of T. W. Wilson

JAY DENNIS

BakerBooks

Grand Rapids

© 2005 by Jay Dennis

Published by Baker Books
a division of Baker Publishing Group
P.O. Box 6287, Grand Rapids, MI 49516-6287
www.bakerbooks.com

Paperback edition published 2007
ISBN 10: 0-8010-6800-2
ISBN 978-0-8010-6800-3

Printed in the United States of America

The Library of Congress has cataloged the hardcover edition as follows:
Dennis, Jay, 1959–
    Leading with Billy Graham : the leadership principles and life of T. W. Wilson/Jay Dennis.
        p.   cm.
    Includes bibliographical references.
    ISBN 10: 0-8010-1251-1
    ISBN 978-0-8010-1251-8
      1. Influence (Psychology)—Religious aspects—Christianity. 2. Wilson, T. W., 1918–
3. Graham, Billy, 1918—Friends and associates. I. Title.
BV4597.53.I52D46 2005
296'.2'092—dc22   2004028608

I dedicate this book
with much love to
Mary Helen Wilson,
Jim Wilson, and Sally Pereira,
along with their families.

CONTENTS

A Personal Word
from Billy Graham

T. W. Wilson was one of the closest and best friends I have ever had. In a wonderful way the Lord knit our souls together, and I do not know what I would have done without his help and encouragement.

We often talked about who would go to heaven first. We talked much about the future life and what it would be like—the friends we would see there and the wonderful fellowship we would have. Most of all, we both looked forward to being with our Lord. T. W. beat me there, and now I'm looking forward to the time when we will be together again.

Billy Graham

ACKNOWLEDGMENTS

I want to thank my incredibly understanding wife, Angie, who has prayed for me, loved me, and encouraged me through this project. This side of heaven she will never know what she means to me. A special thank-you to my administrative assistant, Beth Miller, for her wholehearted dedication, creativity, and endless energy given to this endeavor. A big thank-you to Glenn Wilcox for his tremendous wisdom and insight. Thank you, Vicki Crumpton at Baker Books, for being a fantastic instrument in God's hands to make an impact in the world. Thank you, Billy Graham and the Billy Graham Evangelistic Association, for your great help and encouragement in writing this book, especially to David Bruce for being a true friend.

I am happy to say that T. W. Wilson was my friend and a real mentor for me even in the short time I knew him. He and Mary Helen opened their home and made me family. I had the privilege of being with them at Amsterdam 2000 and spent a wonderful time with them, their family, and their many friends associated with the Billy Graham Evangelistic Association. I interviewed Billy Kim; Bill and Vonette Bright; Luis

Palau; Sir David McNee (former head of Scotland Yard); Dr. Stephen Olford and his wife, Heather; Dr. John R. W. Stott; Dr. Lewis Drummond and his wife, Betty; Millie Dienert; Dr. Richard Bewes; Dr. Jimmy Draper; Glenn Wilcox; Dr. Roger James; and family members, friends, and members of the Billy Graham Evangelistic Association team.[1] Further, I was able on three occasions to spend time with Billy Graham, enjoying his insights into his friend T. W. I noticed a consistent testimony concerning T. W. Without using these words, everyone I spoke with communicated, "T. W. had a next-level influence."

I was privileged to have spent many hours interviewing T. W. and his friends. His influence in my life had a profound impact upon my thinking and my ministry. I wish I had met him twenty years earlier when I was a younger pastor. I hope his life will be an inspiration to you as well.

1

WHAT IS
NEXT-LEVEL INFLUENCE?

Whether a businessperson, a student, a ministry worker, a stay-at-home mom, a retiree—anyone can have next-level influence. It is found equally in men and women. It can be used on any person with whom you are dealing or any group of people. Next-level influence works in any setting.

There is a difference between influence and next-level influence. Influence is basically the attempt to persuade people to do something. That can apply to any area of life. It could come from the real estate agent trying to get someone to buy a home, the car salesman making a pitch to get someone to purchase a car, the corporate headhunter attempting to persuade someone to take another job, the coach attempting to motivate his team, the teacher trying to engage her students to learn, or the commercial attempting to get us to buy a certain product.

Next-level influence, however, has an otherworld dimension to it. It has eternal implications. Next-level influence at its core seeks not to persuade people to a certain action but to persuade them to *a way of thinking.* For the Christian, that persuasion is to a biblical worldview that begins with a relationship with Jesus Christ by faith. As Benjamin Franklin said, "He who shall introduce into public affairs the principles of primitive Christianity, will change the face of the world."[1] Next-level influence's goal is to get people to consider God in their lives.

Next-level influence is seen throughout the Bible. Here are a few examples:

+ Joseph had next-level influence over Pharaoh (Gen. 41:16, 39).
+ Moses had next-level influence over the people of Israel as he led them out of Egypt and through the Red Sea (Exod. 14:13).
+ David had next-level influence as he took on the giant Goliath in the strength of the Lord (1 Sam. 17:45–47).
+ Jonathan, Saul's son, had next-level influence over David, saving his life (1 Sam. 19:1–2).
+ Elijah had next-level influence over the prophets of Baal as the fire fell from heaven in response to his prayers and obedience (1 Kings 18:38–39).
+ Jabez had next-level influence as he committed himself to God's covenant and asked God to expand his influence for God (1 Chron. 4:9–10).
+ Nehemiah had next-level influence with King Artaxerxes who allowed him to go and do the impossible task of re-

building the walls of Jerusalem in fifty-two days (Neh. 2:1–5).

+ Esther had next-level influence with King Artaxerxes and saved the Jewish people (Esth. 7:2–3).

+ Daniel had next-level influence over King Darius and turned the country in a God-ward direction (Dan. 6:25–28).

+ Andrew had next-level influence over his brother Peter and brought him to Christ (John 1:40–42).

+ Barnabas had next-level influence and encouraged the early New Testament church to be givers and servants (Acts 4:36–37; 11:23–26).

+ Stephen, who was the first martyr for the Christian faith, had next-level influence over a young man named Saul as he lay dying after being stoned (Acts 7:58–60).

Countless other biblical and historical examples can be given. "My Country, 'Tis of Thee" was written by Samuel Francis Smith, a Baptist minister. The Pledge of Allegiance was written in 1892 by a Baptist minister named Francis Bellamy. The words "In God We Trust" as an American motto are traced to the efforts of Reverend W. R. Watkinson. One signer of the Declaration of Independence was Reverend John Witherspoon, a Presbyterian minister.[2] And consider this true story:

A young boy by the name of James had a desire to be the most famous manufacturer and salesman of cheese in the world. He planned on becoming rich and famous by making and selling cheese and began with a little buggy pulled by a pony named Paddy. After making his cheese, he would load his wagon, and he and Paddy would drive down the streets of Chicago to sell the cheese. As the months passed, the young boy began to despair because he was not making any money, in spite of his long hours and hard work.

One day he pulled his pony to a stop and began to talk to him. He said, "Paddy, there is something wrong. We are not doing it right. I am afraid we have things turned around and our priorities are not where they ought to be. Maybe we ought to serve God and place him first in our lives." The boy drove home and made a covenant that for the rest of his life he would first serve God and then would work as God directed.

Many years after this, the young boy, now a man, stood as Sunday School Superintendent at North Shore Baptist Church in Chicago and said, "I would rather be a layman in the North Shore Baptist Church than to head the greatest corporation in America. My first job is serving Jesus." So, every time you take a bite of Philadelphia Cream cheese, sip a cup of Maxwell House, mix a quart of Kool-Aid, slice up a DiGiorno Pizza, cook a pot of Macaroni & Cheese, spread some Grey Poupon, stir a bowl of Cream of Wheat, slurp down some Jell-O, eat the cream out of the middle of an Oreo cookie, or serve some Stove Top, remember a boy, his pony named Paddy, and the promise little James L. Kraft made to serve God and work as he directed.[3]

Mel Gibson's movie *The Passion of the Christ* is a next-level influence movie. It got an entire nation talking and thinking about the real Jesus and biblical truth. This Hollywood box-office hit influenced every media outlet from magazines and newspapers to radio talk shows, network talk shows, and cable news. Many churches used this movie as a way to reach out to unbelievers.

Mark Sanborn, in his book *The Fred Factor*, tells the story of his postman of ten years named "Fred" who has next-level influence. His exemplary attitude, consistent go-beyond-what-is-necessary work ethic, ability to anticipate needs and meet those needs, and commitment to excellence caused the author to coin the term "the Fred Factor." It defines one who proactively approaches life with enthusiasm and an "I'm out to change my world" outlook. A postman named Fred changed his world by exceptionally doing his job day in and day out.[4]

Another example of influence is Billy Graham, who has consistently been able to get the world to consider another world. He has preached the gospel message for more than sixty years and has preached to more people than any other person in history. When we hear his name, we think about God. He has pushed our society's thinking in a Christ-ward direction.

In the nineteenth century a famous Methodist evangelist named Peter Cartwright was known for his uncompromising preaching. However, one day when President Andrew Jackson, "Old Hickory," came to Cartwright's church, the elders warned the pastor not to offend the president. In those days, the president had great power to influence a denomination for good or bad. Content that their pastor would not say anything to discredit their church, the elders retired to the back of the sanctuary.

When Cartwright got up to speak, the first words out of his mouth were, "I understand that Andrew Jackson is here this morning. I have been requested to be very guarded in my remarks. Let me say this: Andrew Jackson will go to hell if he doesn't repent of his sin!" The entire congregation gasped with shock at Cartwright's boldness. How could this young preacher dare to offend the tough old general in public? After the service, everyone wondered how the president would respond to Cartwright. When Andrew Jackson met the preacher at the door, he looked him in the eye and said, "Sir, if I had a regiment of men like you, I could conquer the world!"[5]

Without question, however, the greatest next-level influencer who has ever lived is Jesus Christ. His life, death, and resurrection changed history and even altered our calendar so that we date our years by his birth. The powerful words of "One Solitary Life" beautifully communicate Jesus's next-level influence.

> He was born in an obscure village, the child of a peasant woman. He worked in a carpentry shop until he was thirty, and then for three years he was an itinerant preacher. When the tide of popular opinion turned against him, his friends ran away. He was turned over to his enemies. He was tried and convicted. He was nailed upon a cross between two thieves. When he was dead, he was laid in a borrowed grave. He never wrote a book. He never held an office. He never owned a home. He never went to college. He never traveled more than two hundred miles from the place where he was born. He never did one of the things that usually accompanies greatness. Yet all the armies that ever marched, and all the governments that ever sat, and all the kings that ever reigned, have not affected life upon this earth as powerfully as has that One Solitary Life.[6]

Historian Phillip Schaff said, "This Jesus of Nazareth, without money and arms, conquered more millions than Alexander, Caesar, Mohammed, and Napoleon; without science . . . he shed more light on things human and divine than all philosophers and scholars combined; without the eloquence of schools, he spoke such words of life as were never spoken before or since and produced effects which lie beyond the reach of orator or poet; without writing a single line, he set more pens in motion and furnished themes for more sermons, orations, discussions, learned volumes, works of art, and songs of praise than the whole army of great men of ancient and modern times."[7]

The impact of this one man can be seen in the hospitals that have been built, the schools and universities that have been started, and the compassionate organizations and programs to reach out to the poor, injured, hurting, and homeless that have been started in his name. He elevated womanhood to its highest level and inspired people to found orphanages for children who have no homes. The list could continue. When Christ lives within us, his resurrection power allows us to have next-level influence.

You may not initially recognize T. W. Wilson's name, but you do recognize the name of Billy Graham. For almost forty years T. W. Wilson was Mr. Graham's best friend, traveling companion, bodyguard, and executive assistant, handling every detail of his demanding schedule. Their friendship began when they were teenagers growing up in Charlotte, North Carolina. You will be fascinated and encouraged by T. W.'s next-level influence whether dealing with presidents or prisoners; celebrities or caretakers; princes or preachers. As you read these stories you will see the sovereignty of God and how he opens doors of influence for us as we are faithful to walk in his will.

In 1858, a Sunday school teacher named Edward Kimball walked into a shoe store in Boston and won a young shoe clerk to faith in Jesus Christ. The clerk's name was D. L. Moody. He became one of the greatest evangelists in American history. Moody traveled to England, where he awakened evangelistic zeal in the heart of a young pastor named F. B. Meyer. In turn, F. B. Meyer became one of the great Bible expositors of all times.

Eventually his ministry brought him to the United States to preach on college campuses.

In one of Meyer's crusades, a student named J. Wilbur Chapman was converted to faith in Christ. While a student at Lake Forest College in the late 1870's, Chapman attended one of D. L. Moody's crusades. Mr. Moody helped him nail down the certainty of his salvation. Then J. Wilbur Chapman became a great preacher and a co-worker of Moody's and carried on an effective work through the YMCA. In his work Chapman employed an ex-baseball player named Billy Sunday as his assistant. He helped organize Chapman's evangelistic meetings.

In time, Billy Sunday became one of America's foremost evangelists. As a result of a crusade Billy Sunday preached in Charlotte, North Carolina, a local group of men, known as the Billy Sunday Layman's Evangelistic Club, was so stirred spiritually that they planned a similar crusade in that city the following year. The group was renamed the Christian Men's Club and was later called the Charlotte Business Men's Committee.

Mordecai Ham was invited to be the evangelist for that meeting. One night during the revival meeting, Billy Graham gave his heart to Christ, and T. W. Wilson and his brother Grady were also touched by God. Their fathers were both part of that committee—two of seven men who knelt in Mr. Graham's cow pasture and prayed for God to raise up a preacher of the gospel.[8]

From that time on, T. W. Wilson began to grow in next-level influence. In 1959, he led a tour group to Israel. While at Jesus's tomb, T. W. was overcome with emotion. God was truly at work. Present was a tour guide named Gabriel Khano, who gave his life to Christ. He said, "I have guided many tours, but this is the first time I have ever seen the risen Jesus." It is one example

among many of T. W.'s next-level influence. He lived by three
principles: 1) read the Bible while you can; 2) go to church in
pain or not; and 3) walk and exercise every day.

On Memorial Day weekend 2004 (the third anniversary of
T. W. Wilson's memorial service), Mary Helen Wilson received
a call from a Dr. Robinson. He had called the Cove—the Billy
Graham Training Center, near Asheville, North Carolina—and
asked how he could reach her. Someone took his number and
passed it on to Mary Helen. She didn't know any Dr. Robinson
but decided she would call him. To her pleasant surprise, it was
Robert Earl Robinson, the son of Mildred Robinson, who had
been the Wilsons' maid many years earlier in Dothan, Alabama.
Dr. Robinson was calling her to share his utmost gratefulness for
what T. W. Wilson had meant to him. As a child, Dr. Robinson
had made many visits with his mother to the Wilsons' home.
The Wilsons also spent much time in the Robinsons' home.

T. W.'s next-level influence affected this African-American
man who now has an earned doctorate and is a prominent pastor in Washington, D.C. He said,

> The unique thing about T. W. Wilson was that, it appeared to
> me, his personality just VIBRATED! It was so alluring to be
> around him. His very demeanor, his smile, his laughter were
> so compelling. In my mind, as I look back, he was part poet,
> part saint. He was a great humanitarian and a good and decent
> man who was concerned about the welfare of others. One time
> when he returned from a crusade overseas, I believe in the Holy
> Land, he came by the house to bring "Little Robert" a slingshot
> just like David used when he slayed the giant Goliath. I carried
> that slingshot with me for years. There is a quote I heard that
> describes T. W. Wilson to me. It is, "What you are speaks so

loudly that sometimes people can't hear what you're saying." What T. W. Wilson was spoke so loudly that he didn't have to say anything.[9]

This book explores eleven principles of next-level influence. You will read stories of T. W. Wilson's next-level influence with Billy Graham and others. These will be followed by specific principles of next-level influence that you can apply to your life and circumstances.

2

WHO WAS
T. W. WILSON?

Thomas Walter "T. W." Wilson served as executive assistant to Billy Graham from 1962 to 2000. He was Billy's bodyguard, traveling companion, accountability partner, and consummate detail man for every aspect of Mr. Graham's ministry. Their relationship began while he and Billy were teenagers growing up in Charlotte, North Carolina. T. W. also served as a pastor and an exceptionally gifted evangelist with the Youth for Christ organization, later becoming an independent evangelist holding crusades around the world.

Between the time of his serving with Youth for Christ and his becoming a part of the Billy Graham Evangelistic Association, T. W. was vice president of Northwestern Schools in Minneapolis, Minnesota, from 1948 to 1951. Billy Graham was the president and enthusiastically asked T. W. to serve with him. T. W.'s filling that position allowed Billy Graham to continue his itinerant ministry of evangelism. It was the beginning of a ministry with Mr. Graham that would last for almost four decades.

In 1999, T. W. had a debilitating stroke, putting an end to his travel with Mr. Graham. Yet "T," as his friends affectionately called him, refused to give up. He lived to be able to share these behind-the-scenes stories of his days with Billy Graham. His insight was priceless, his humor contagious, his presence powerful, his humility attractive, and his discernment unquestioned.

T. W. tells his story: "As a boy I grew up in Charlotte, North Carolina. My father was a Presbyterian; my mother had been a Methodist. When I was born I was premature, and the doctor suggested that my parents just let me die. My parents thought differently. My mother told the doctor, 'If God takes him, that's one thing, but we're not God.' The neighbors heated up bricks in order to keep me warm. Obviously, I greatly value the sanctity of human life.

"Both my parents were wonderful Christians and godly examples. I couldn't have asked for a better environment. When I was a child growing up, my parents were extremely poor. When I was five years old, I got a job with *Liberty* magazine, which is out of existence now. I always managed to have some kind of job, sometimes several jobs at the same time. It would be illegal for children today to work like I had to work.

"Although I had godly parents, I didn't live what I knew to be best. I was a typical unconverted boy even though I learned the Shorter Catechism when I was twelve years old. The church that I went to was not a very good church. The Sunday school teacher said, 'It's all right to take a little drink once in a while if you don't run it in the ground.' In that particular Sunday school class these young kids would smoke cigarettes while the teacher was teaching the class. Sometimes the teacher would smoke his cigarettes. So the church wasn't a very wholesome environment. Most of my friends were not Christians, not exemplary in any way.

"But when I was fourteen years old I met Billy Graham. I met his father and mother and they were two of the most saintly, godly people I ever met in my life. Mrs. Graham had been a schoolteacher; Mr. Graham was a farmer. Dr. Mordecai Ham came to Charlotte, North Carolina, for revival meetings. My father was on the committee that brought him to the city. They built a special tabernacle. My late brother Grady and Billy sang in the choir. I say 'sang in the choir'; they really 'sat' in the choir. Billy was not a great singer; Grady was better than the two of us. I think they sat in the choir to keep Dr. Ham from pointing his finger at them. He stirred up all kinds of things in Charlotte. This was probably the beginning of Grady, Billy, and me being exposed to real biblical truth.

"My experience of becoming a Christian was quite unusual and different. My mother and father had set the right example. They took me to hear every preacher that came to Charlotte, and I was disgusted with all of them simply because I was under conviction.

"One night I went to a revival meeting, and during the invitation to accept Christ I saw a young man that later I came to know as a real man of God walking down the aisle asking different young people if they were Christians. I saw him looking in my direction, and I was seated on the back row of the tent. When I saw him just two rows from me, looking straight at me, I whirled out of the tent. I wasn't going to let him try to get religion down my throat. So I ran out of that revival meeting to keep from having that man put the bee on me.

"Two blocks away from the tent I thought I was going to die, I was under such mighty conviction. I found it difficult to get my breath and finally I said, 'O God, please help me. I'm going to die.' In an open field, with white flannel trousers and a blue coat on, I lay down on my stomach and begged God to please do something to help me. Right then he seemed to say to me, 'Have you asked me to save you?' And I said, 'Lord, whatever it takes, please save me.'

"I walked home. My parents were already there and my mother said, 'Son, where were you tonight? We looked around and didn't see you.' I told her I decided to walk home and on the way home I met a wild, rough cousin who said, 'T, we haven't seen you in several days. Come on with me.' And he told me where he wanted to go, and I knew it was not a place I ought to be, so I went on toward home.

"Usually they had to drag me out of bed, but that next morning I woke up. I had never gotten up early before. I got up and got the Bible and went into the living room. Nobody else was awake at that time. So I started reading the Bible, and I opened to the book of Matthew with all the 'begats' and I said, 'O God, I can't understand this stuff.' And it just seemed like the Holy Spirit led me to flip over to the Gospel of John, and I was reading it and understanding it little by little.

"While I was reading my mother came down the stairs. I heard her coming, so I put the Bible under a pillow on the sofa. I was just sitting there, and she said, 'Son, what's different about you? Why are you up so early?' I said, 'Oh, I just decided to get up early this morning.' So she went on through the dining room to the kitchen, and I heard her whistling. I decided to get the Bible and start reading it again.

"This time I was getting something out of reading the Gospel of John. It was so interesting to me that all of a sudden I looked up and saw my mother. I hadn't heard her come in, and she said, 'Son, what are you doing?' I said, 'Oh, Mother, I just decided to get up early and read this morning.' Then she said, 'Son, have you been converted?' And I said, 'Yes ma'am.' Then Mother came over and hugged me, knelt beside me and prayed for me. That was the beginning of my Christian life.

"Although I was sprinkled as a child, I went to college and had begun to study the Bible, and I felt in my heart I needed to be baptized by immersion. I was a student at Bob Jones College in Cleveland, Tennessee. I went over to Chattanooga to see pastor T. W. Calloway and I told him I believed the Bible teaches baptism by immersion. I was baptized in the St. Elmo Baptist Church in Chattanooga, and later I was ordained to preach the gospel in that same church on May 31, 1939. I took my first pastorate on October 1, 1942. While I was in college I got to know a graduate of Bob Jones College by the name of Jimmie Johnson, who had gotten me interested in going to college. He helped me financially while I was in school and was very instrumental in the development of my Christian experience in those early days. Our first child, a son, was named after Jimmie.

"At Bob Jones College I met a young lady by the name of Mary Helen Sellers. We began dating, and I fell in love with her. I felt like she was the one for me, but I wasn't sure, even though I loved her very much. I asked her one night, 'If God called me to preach and I had to go to another country as a missionary and be away from loved ones, would you be willing to go with me?' She looked me straight in the eye and said, 'I'll go with you wherever you believe God wants you to go.' We dated a year before we were married in the First Baptist Church of Dothan, Alabama. My late brother Grady was my best man.

"I pastored two churches—the Grandview Baptist Church in Dothan, Alabama, and First Baptist Church, Ashburn, Georgia. After pastoring, I preached all over the United States and other countries under Youth for Christ International. I became Vice President At-Large. After I left that position, I held crusades all over the country at the same time Billy Graham was having crusades on his own. From 1948 until 1951 I accepted Billy's call to go with him to Northwestern Schools in Minneapolis, Minnesota. From 1952 to 1956, I was an independent evangelist.

"In 1956, things were about to change forever for me. I joined the Billy Graham Evangelistic Association, and I have never left. Billy asked me to become his executive assistant, and I have joyfully spent my life serving the Lord by serving Billy Graham."

T. W. would take his brother Grady's place in this position when Grady's health prevented him from keeping up the strenuous schedule. T. W. recalled, "Grady and I were the closest of any family members, and of course we enjoyed working together. His sense of humor had a purpose, and on occasions he would just tell jokes for the joke's sake. He had probably as many friends in the Billy Graham organization as any other person. Billy trusted his insight. He was always straightforward with Billy, as I have tried to be. There was never any political motivation with Grady and me. He was a straight shooter and a very competent preacher and evangelist. He was my pal, and

I had great admiration for him. He was full of humor, yet he had a deep seriousness and spiritual commitment—a rare combination. Grady was fourteen months younger than I, yet he has been dead since 1987. I still miss him, and I'm sure that Billy Graham and the whole team miss him."

As T. W. and Grady Wilson's dad lay dying, the brothers were with him. What their father had taught them by example through the years and what he said to them in his final moments on earth greatly impacted both of them. T. W. shared this story:

"Daddy was an old plumber and a hard worker. He had been battling cancer and was in a coma. We didn't think he was going to revive at all. Grady and I were sitting in the room. All of a sudden Daddy's eyes started to flicker, and Grady said, 'T, Daddy is going to wake up.'

"So we both rushed over to each side of the bed. Sure enough, his eyes did open. I said, 'Daddy, would you like to pray?'

"He reached out and got both our hands and he just raised them up, and said, '*Dear Lord, help my boys to preach the gospel.*' And then he died."

The widow of famed evangelist Billy Sunday gave T. W. a book entitled *Billy Sunday: The Man and His Message* by William T. Ellis.[1] She inscribed the book, "To my friend, T. W. Wilson, from Mrs. W. A. (Ma) Sunday, Isaiah 41:10, June 3, 1941, Be yourself, preach the Word, be much in prayer—W. A. Sunday." T. W. Wilson lived up to those words.

T. W. has been called "the real deal," "authentic," and "transparent." He's been labeled the "Velcro person" for holding everything together and picking up the loose ends. He has also been called "the gatekeeper" to Billy Graham. He perfectly exemplifies next-level influence.

This man influenced everyone with whom he came in contact. I am fortunate to have had the opportunity to become friends with this giant of the faith. Knowing him has deepened my own belief that next-level influence can be more than a dream. On May 24, 2001, T. W. Wilson went home to heaven. Heaven gained a giant as the world lost a next-level influencer, yet his influence lives on through the lives he touched.

3

SPIRITUAL MILE MARKERS

Next-Level Influencers
Look Back

You see them on every highway and interstate system: mile markers. Small signs with numbers give a point of reference as to where you are, where you have been, and where you are going. Birthdays do the same thing. Every birthday is another mile marker or year marker on life's journey. Each of us can look back and see specific times and occasions when something happened to change our direction, our perspective, and perhaps our future. These mile markers often occur without fanfare or "ta-da's." Yet when we look back we see that on a certain day something significant happened.

The most influential spiritual mile marker is salvation, where one becomes a new creation through a relationship with Jesus Christ. Although the process by which one comes to Christ is different for each person, the way a person is saved remains the same for everyone. Next-level influence occurred in our lives when a person (a parent, friend, co-worker) or a group of people (a church, a Christian organization, a small group) shared with us how to have a relationship with Jesus.

Spiritual mile markers normally take place on ordinary, sometimes even mundane days. Call them "divine appointments," "God's setups," or "God's interruptions," but one thing is certain, God is at work all of the time all around us. As Henry Blackaby suggests in his Bible study, *Experiencing God*, "Watch to see where God is working and join Him!"[1] God graciously invites us to become a part of what he is doing.

"Evangelist to the world" Billy Graham has certainly experienced numerous mile markers, from people he has met to crusades where he has preached, places he has visited, and things he has said or done that God used. Billy Graham and T. W. Wilson shared a number of spiritual mile markers.

T. W. Wilson allows us to get a perspective of how God orchestrated these life-changing moments. His insights into the details are a blessing and encouragement to the kingdom of God. Since he was a behind-the-scenes person, his contribution could easily be missed. But his is exactly the kind of influence of which we all need to be reminded.

Mordecai Ham and the Crusade That Almost Wasn't

T. W. Wilson's relationship with Billy Graham goes back to their early teenage years. We often hear Mordecai Ham's name associated with Billy Graham's becoming a Christian. T. W.'s version of this 1934 crusade in Charlotte, North Carolina, offers a viewpoint that many may not know. This was perhaps the most significant mile marker in Billy Graham, T. W. Wilson, and Grady Wilson's lives. T. W. told the story: "When I was first converted, I was a senior in Central High in Charlotte, North Carolina. When Mordecai Ham came to Charlotte for a crusade, I had already made my commitment in a way, but Grady, my brother, and Billy sang in the choir. Now, Billy can't sing. He'd be the first one to admit it if he was honest. He can't sing. But he and Grady sang in the choir and stayed in the choir. Grady could at least sing.

"I would look up at them, and they wouldn't dare look at me, because they knew what I was thinking—'You're up there looking out in the audience for girls or because you don't want Dr. Ham to point his finger at you. What are you doing up there? You can't sing!'

"But that was a turning point, the Mordecai Ham campaign, for all three of us. That's where Grady and Billy and I became such close friends . . . because my father and Billy's were some of the leaders of the Mordecai Ham meetings. They lasted about three or four weeks. We went mainly because our folks wanted us to go. My father was on the committee.

"That's really the first time that Grady and Billy and I, all three, really got an appreciation for an evangelist. Dr. Ham was so forthright, and he would call a spade a spade, and he was pointing out the trouble facing young people. One night the ringleader of the 'atheist' club in our high school, Central High in Charlotte, got a whole bunch of these so-called atheists, and they came in on the side of the tabernacle. [Note: A tabernacle is a wooden-framed structure with canvas on the top and sawdust on the floor.] They came marching in, and I shall never forget it.

"The ushers had been tipped off that the atheists were coming in. So as they marched in, Alvin Whitfield, a little, short fellow who was an atheist, came down and said, 'Now look-a-here, Ham.' There was a great big usher—I don't know if he was the chief usher or what, but he just picked him up on his shoulder, like you would pick up a little baby. The other ushers said, 'This way, please . . .' and marched them right on out. And so it was noised about to come see this 'fightin' preacher.

"So one night we were all looking forward to hearing Dr. Ham, but he didn't come, and Mr. Treadway, the song director, said, 'I don't know what has happened to Dr. Ham, but I'm surprised he is not here.' Well, what happened was that the principal of the high school, who wasn't a believer, and some others made a deal with the newspapers. They planned to embarrass Dr. Ham and have a woman come to his hotel room. As soon as he opened the door, she was going to grab him and hug him, and then this newspaper photographer was going to take a picture.

"A godly secretary had overheard the plans of this newspaper man and the photographer, and she called and talked to either my father or one of the other leaders of the crusade.

"So my father and Mr. Banks Reed waited in a hotel room across the hall and foiled the plan by running into the hall and yelling, 'What are you doing?' And they spoiled the whole thing. All of that came out in the paper.

"This one particular night, as he was on his way to Charlotte, some men who didn't want to see the crusade come to town locked Dr. Ham up in the restroom of the train. The first stop after leaving Charlotte was Spartanburg, and he couldn't get out, and then when he did get out, they couldn't stop the train, and he said, 'Yes, but I'm a minister and I have to get to Charlotte where I am preaching.' They let him out in Spartanburg. He didn't have a car or anything, so he got a taxi in Spartanburg to take him straight to the meeting. When we heard about this fighting Baptist preacher, that's when we got interested. That's when Billy and Grady and I became such good friends. I was about fifteen or sixteen years old."

At this crusade Billy Graham gave his heart to Jesus Christ. It was also when God began to focus T. W. on what would become his life calling. No wonder Satan tried his best to derail this eternally significant meeting. Praying people brought the breakthrough.

The Meeting That Launched a Legacy

Fast-forward to the great 1949 Los Angeles crusade. Arguably, this was the crusade that launched Billy Graham into worldwide prominence. That meeting lasted longer than anyone could have predicted. Billy called T. W. and said, "Bring sermons." The atmosphere was electric with anticipation. T. W. recalled, "Billy asked me to preach for him. I was scared, but I did it anyway. I remember when I first got up and started to pray, there was a voice and a fellow [walking] down the aisle. He thought I was Billy; he said, 'Oh, Billy Graham, I'm a drunk, I'm lost, and I need to be saved.' So I said, 'Well, God bless you, sir. Come on down here, anybody else? This man said he needs to be saved. We don't need a sermon; we just need to pray. Maybe there's somebody else who needs to be saved. You come on.' There were almost thirty that came down and wanted to be saved right then, before any sermon or anything. That was a night when the Holy Spirit was doing his work."

In another instance, T. W. recounted, "During the 1949 crusade in Los Angeles with Billy, people started coming in and stayed overnight, because they were afraid they wouldn't be there for the closing of the crusade on Sunday afternoon. So about 10:00 a.m. that Sunday morning, this man, who was the custodian of the tent, saw all those people there. He was not a preacher, but he was a great Christian, and he loved the Lord, and so he went out and he turned on the public address system. He said, 'Folks, I'm not a preacher or the son of a preacher. But I'm a Christian, I love the Lord, and you know, most people are in Sunday school somewhere. If you don't mind, I'd just like to read you a few Scripture verses and tell you what the Lord means to me.' And he gave an invitation and right there twenty-seven people made a decision for Christ."

God's Timing Is Everything

T. W. Wilson was having great success as an evangelist. For years he, along with Cliff Barrows, Chuck Templeton, and Billy Graham, had been used by God to see thousands come to Christ through Youth for Christ under the leadership of Torrey Johnson. Cliff and T. W. had been inducted into Youth for Christ on the same day. Cliff Barrows recounts, "I graduated in 1944. Our paths crossed again in 1945, because he and I both went into Youth for Christ at the same time. At the same executive committee meeting, they voted to accept T. W. and me as field evangelists, out in Los Angeles. They didn't know whether they wanted this Southern boy and this boy from California, because I was from the West Coast, or not. T had really had some very effective meetings with young people. He was a good communicator. He preached with passion."

But things were about to drastically change for T. W. and for Billy Graham. Grady Wilson, Billy's executive assistant and T. W.'s brother, began to hold crusades of his own, so Billy tried to persuade T. W. to take Grady's place. When Billy Graham approached T. W. about becoming his executive assistant, T. W. was concerned that he wouldn't get to preach as much. Billy said that this was true and then asked, "T, are you more interested in how many times you can preach or how much you can do for God?" That got T. W.'s attention.

Glenn Wilcox, a longtime friend and confidant of T. W., shared the humorous encounter between Billy and T. W. about T. W. becoming the evangelist's executive assistant. The two men were traveling together when Billy Graham came to T. W.—in the wee hours of the morning—to share with him what the Lord had laid on his heart. As Glenn Wilcox tells it, "It was about three o'clock in the morning and [Billy] woke [T. W.] up. He came into his room; they were in separate rooms. He said, 'T, I want to talk to you about something.'

"[T. W.] said, 'Billy, it's three o'clock in the morning—can't you wait until breakfast to talk to me?'

"[Billy] said, 'No, God told me you need to be my administrative assistant and travel with me.'

"[T. W.] said, 'God told you what?' And then he said, best I can remember, 'Well, God didn't tell me.'

"[Billy] said, 'Well, will you pray about it?'

"[T. W.] said, 'I don't need to pray about it.'

"[Billy] said, 'Write that down—you don't need to pray about it.'

"And so [T. W.] said, 'Look, Billy, you go on back to your room. I'm going to bed. You pray about this. I'm going to go back to sleep.'

"I think [T. W.] called Mary Helen [T. W.'s wife], and Mary Helen said, 'Darling, whatever you decide I will accept. Just be sure you are in God's will, because if you're not, you will be miserable and the family will be also.'

"So, the next morning Ruth [Graham] came in and said, 'T, I want to talk to you.'

"[T. W.] said, 'Okay.'

"[Ruth] said, 'Will you not take the job because you're afraid of me interfering?' (Which was a pretty good question that shows that she is an incredibly sensitive woman. I mean, to travel with him all the time, and be with him, [he would] have to be involved with her too.) [Ruth] said, 'I want you to know, I will never interfere. I will not do anything.' And he let her talk about forty-five minutes, you know. And then she says, 'Well, why won't you do it?' And [T. W.] says, 'Well, I'm going to do it. I had already made my mind up . . .' [To which Ruth responded:] 'And you let me talk for forty-five minutes!'

"After the crusade that night Billy said to T. W., 'Ruth said the two of you had a good visit this afternoon.' Finally Ruth said, 'T, what he is talking about is what you shared with me about going with him full-time.' Billy said, 'Well, praise God, I knew you were going to do it.' T. W. said, 'Well, I didn't.'"

As William Martin said, "Over the next thirty years, no one, including Ruth, would spend more time at Billy's side than T. W. Wilson."[2] Martin also said:

Since that afternoon in 1962, T. W. Wilson has spent most days of his life at the side of or within easy reach of Billy Graham, serving as his gatekeeper, travel agent, valet, nurse, adviser, buffer, booster, defender, listener, jollier, minesweeper, and constant chaperon. Colleagues and knowledgeable observers of the Graham organization alike almost invariably describe him as "an amazing man," "one of the strong backbones of the entire association," "a man who is able to subordinate himself without ever worrying about it a minute," and "a man who knows how to take care of Billy without making everybody mad."[3]

The Beginnings of Campus Crusade for Christ

Billy and T. W. influenced Bill and Vonette Bright, especially in the early years of their ministry. One night after the Los Angeles crusade, the Brights invited Billy and some of the other team members to their home. T. W. gave his version of that significant moment: "We were there for dinner that night after the crusade. Bill Bright said to Billy in my hearing, 'Billy, I really don't know what to do with my life. I love the Lord, but I don't know whether I should try to get a pastorate. I just don't know. Do you have any suggestions?'

"And Billy said, 'Bill, what are you interested in more than anything else?' He looked at Vonette, and he said, 'Well, I think that we're interested more in students than anything else.' Billy said, 'Then why don't you give your life for students?' He looked at Vonette and he said, 'That's something to pray about.' Billy gave the first gift that night to what would become Campus Crusade for Christ."

That organization is now the largest Christian ministry in the world. Campus Crusade for Christ serves people in 191 countries through a staff of 26,000 full-time employees and more than 225,000 trained volunteers working in some 60 different ministries and projects. Bill Bright wrote a booklet called *The Four Spiritual Laws*, which has been printed in 200 languages and distributed to more than 2.5 billion people—making it the most widely distributed religious booklet in history. In 1979, Bill Bright commissioned the *Jesus* film that has been viewed by more than 5.1 billion people in 234 countries and has become the most widely viewed, as well as most widely translated, film in history.[4] Bill Bright experienced and practiced next-level influence.

The Seoul Crusade

When asked what stood out in his mind from all his years of working with Billy Graham, without hesitation T. W. said, "The 1973 Seoul, Korea, crusade. Never have I heard Billy Graham preach better and felt the power of the Holy Spirit coming on a crusade more than in that crusade. Over 1.2 million people gathered in Yoido Plaza to hear the gospel." Billy Graham echoed the same sentiment. Anyone who was there simply had never experienced anything like it before. Sitting by Ruth Graham on the platform, T. W. said, "Ruth, how would you describe it?" She said, "T. W., I'm looking at it, and I can't believe it myself."

At the end of the last service, Billy Graham and T. W. Wilson got into a military helicopter and exited the plaza. T. W. said that as the chopper made its way to the airport, he looked down and saw the most incredible sight he had ever experienced. All of those Koreans who had been through so very much living in the constant tension of war were waving their white handkerchiefs as a way of saying, "Thank you, Billy Graham; thank you, Jesus!" This spiritual mile marker has had multiple ramifications for the kingdom of God and for the country of South Korea. Many believe that the megachurch movement in that country started with this crusade.

The Power of Spiritual Mile Markers

Spiritual mile markers like these have influenced history. Although there will never be another Billy Graham and T. W. Wilson, we have many opportunities to become next-level influencers wherever God has called us.

Next-level influencers look back and see how God has directed their steps, orchestrated their schedules, and allowed them to experience certain things in order to make them more usable and more influential. They do not waste any experience, whether good or bad. Looking back allows us to see those times when we were in God's will and those times when unfortunately we were not. God's will is often seen more clearly by looking in life's rearview mirror.

President Ronald Reagan said, "I've often wondered at how lives are shaped by what seem like small and inconsequential events, how an apparently random turn in the road can lead you a long way from where you intend to go—a long way from wherever you expected to go."[5]

Consider the following lessons on next-level influence.

1. Your Only Assignment Is to Be in God's Will at All Times

We never know where the will of God will take us or what experiences it will bring us. But the passion of our lives must always be to stay in the center of God's will. When we do, we discover we do not need to attempt to manipulate things, make things happen, orchestrate circumstances, or force things to happen as a result of our own efforts. As we seek only to do the Father's will, we start to live in the arena of God's activity, the place where things are happening. Divine appointments—those people you "happen" to run into because God set it up—take place most often in your daily routine.

The place of maximum influence emerges at the point of our "yes" to his will. Providing us with those divine connections then becomes God's responsibility, not ours. "To know the will of God is the greatest knowledge. To do the will of God is the greatest achievement."[6]

What a relief to know that once we obey God, we can turn our day over to him. Availability to God through continually walking in his will often leads to next-level influence with someone. That makes living the Christian life the most exciting adventure known to the human spirit.

2. Trust God's Timing

God is on time, always, without exception. His sovereignty is the standard time. We adjust our clocks to his. That means we don't get ahead of God by taking matters into our own hands and also suggests that we wait until God says "Go for it" before we move out. God's timing creates the environment for real influence to happen. As you look back at situations you have faced, you no doubt see now how God came through just in the nick of time.

That is what the writer of Hebrews was suggesting when he said, "Therefore let us draw near with confidence to the throne of grace, so that we may receive mercy and find grace to help in time of need" (Heb. 4:16). As W. Glyn Evans said,

"God must reserve for Himself the right of the initiative, the right to break into my life without question or explanation. That shattering phone call, that disturbing letter may indeed be the first stage of God's interruption in my life. . . . Since God does the initiating, He must be responsible for the consequences."[7] We are not to worry about God's timing. As we continue in God's will, he makes sure we are at the right place at the right time.

3. God Often Uses Improbable People

Next-level influencers don't have to be from the "Who's Who" of life. People who most influence the world often come from improbable places and families. God does not base his using someone to influence the world on brains, brawn, bucks, or beauty. Scripture says, "Take a good look, friends, at who you were when you got called into this life. I don't see many of 'the brightest and the best' among you, not many influential, not many from high-society families. Isn't it obvious that God deliberately chose men and women that the culture overlooks and exploits and abuses, chose these 'nobodies' to expose the hollow pretensions of the 'somebodies'? That makes it quite clear that none of you can get by with blowing your own horn before God. Everything that we have—right thinking and right living, a clean slate and a fresh start—comes from God by way of Jesus Christ. That's why we have the saying, 'If you're going to blow a horn, blow a trumpet for God'" (1 Cor. 1:26–31 Message).

T. W. Wilson was a highly unlikely person, in the world's eyes, to have influenced so many people, especially those in places of great authority. He didn't seek that; he was simply available to be used by God. The qualities God looks for are faith, purity, holiness, and obedience—those things to which the world is blinded when it looks for its choice. Anyone possessing those qualities becomes a candidate for a next-level influencer. What Samuel said of God concerning a young, unlikely David becoming the King of Israel is still relevant for today: "God sees not as man sees, for man looks at the outward appearance, but the LORD looks at the heart" (1 Sam. 16:7). In other words, "God does not always choose great people to accomplish what he wishes, but he chooses a person who is wholly yielded to him."[8]

4. You Never Know What One Word or Action Done in Jesus's Name Will Do

Think about something someone said to you or did for you that became a spiritual benchmark for you—something God used to influence you. Just a word from Billy Graham to a young Bill Bright encouraged the beginning of Campus Crusade for Christ, a ministry that is touching the world with the gospel message.

Consider the committee of men who decided to invite Mordecai Ham to conduct a crusade in Charlotte, North Carolina, or the actions of a secretary who overheard an evil plot against Reverend Ham. All of this may not have seemed eternally significant at the time, but it had eternal consequences. God may use a word of encouragement, a prayer for someone, or simply a smile to influence a person's life. You may not immediately see it, or you may not ever see it at all, but perhaps you will be able to look back and see something that changed the course of events or changed a person's life. "Keep on sowing your seed, for you never know which will grow—perhaps it all will" (Eccles. 11:6 TLB).

5. Building Relationships Is Vital to Kingdom Effectiveness

The word *relationship* may be the most important word in our language. Dietrich Bonhoeffer said, "There is hardly anything that can make one happier than to feel that one counts for something with other people. What matters here is not numbers, but intensity. In the long run, human relationships are the most important thing in life."[9]

The kingdom of God is influenced through relationships. Building relationships means you invest time and energy in people. You value another person and desire to devote yourself to that person. Relationships are often inconvenient, yet it is precisely through relationships that we influence people. I am not suggesting you try to get to know somebody for what that person can do for you. It is embarrassing to watch some people work to get close to someone important in order to take advantage for personal reasons. Building relationships means taking the initiative to love people, spend time with them, encourage them, and show concern for them.

Billy Graham certainly recognized the importance of a relationship. He knew he couldn't do what God had called him to do alone. He needed T. W. Wilson. Next-level influencers are aware they need others. They avoid a "lone ranger" attitude. Their strength of character allows them to admit, "I can't do this by myself." The kingdom of God is about being connected with others. Next-level influencers surround themselves with the very best people, then listen to them, learn from them, and make them a part of the process.

6. *Don't Forget Those Spiritual Mile Markers in Your Life*

Some earthly encounters have only a heavenly explanation. Look back and realize that what has happened in your life was from the hand of God. Your life is made up of the experiences you have had and the people you have met. Charlie "Tremendous" Jones says, "You are the same person five years from now except for two things . . . the people you meet and the books you read."[10]

Some times in your life didn't seem at the moment to be of great significance, yet God used them to change your direction, your future, and perhaps even your destiny. A "chance" meeting, a delayed flight, a perceived interruption may be the very thing that changes you or changes others through you. As a next-level influencer, you can be the person God uses as a spiritual mile marker in someone else's life.

Through the process of writing this book I have formed some lifelong friendships. One of those relationships is with Billy Kim, whom I call "the Billy Graham of Southeast Asia." My first meeting with him in Amsterdam in the summer of 2000 was a spiritual mile marker. I saw him again in June of 2001. My wife, Angie, and I were at the Southern Baptist Convention in New Orleans. Prior to leaving our hotel room one afternoon, we paused and prayed that God would bring us a divine appointment. As we were walking down the corridor, I saw Billy Kim walking by himself. This was to be our divine appointment. I asked him if we could take him to dinner the next evening. We did, and over a meal he asked me to come to Korea later that summer to preach in his great church and assist him in baptizing approximately four thousand Korean soldiers who had come to Christ.

In January of 2003, he asked me to come back to preach again and speak at the first Far East Broadcasting Company convention. My Tae Kwon Do instructor in Lakeland, Florida, Grand Master Sun Took Choe, had a niece from Seoul who moved in with him and his wife to go to Lakeland Christian School. Knowing that I was going to preach in Seoul, Master Choe contacted his niece's parents in Korea and asked them to come hear me preach. During the invitation that Sunday morning, both of her parents received Christ. They were Buddhists and had never heard the gospel. Looking back, it was a heavenly encounter with no earthly explanation—that all came out of meeting Billy Kim during an interview for this book. Watch and see what God does with your seemingly ordinary encounters too!

4

"HELLO, MR. PRESIDENT"

Next-Level Influencers
Seize Divine Appointments

When Billy Graham was pastor at Western Springs Baptist Church in Western Springs, Illinois, he wrote teasingly to T. W., "I think it is a shame that we 'big' preachers don't keep in contact any more than we do, because when we do whip Germany, Mr. Roosevelt won't know where to get in touch with us in order for us to settle the peace."[1] At that moment it was a joke, but in years to come, influencing presidents would become reality.

T. W. Wilson's relationship and position with Billy Graham gave him the privilege of meeting and spending significant time with several presidents of the United States. Not one to seek the limelight, T. W.'s humble spirit and friendliness caught the attention of more than one president. God simply opened a window of opportunity and allowed T. W. to get a glimpse into the spiritual lives of the leaders of the free world and sometimes even into the lives of future presidents.

Lyndon B. Johnson

Consider this incident between President Lyndon Baines Johnson and T. W. Wilson:

> When President Johnson was recuperating at Charlottesville, Virginia, after a heart attack, T. W. Wilson stayed dutifully outside when Billy went in. A few minutes later the Secret Service man summoned him. "T. W.," said the president, "I thought you came here to see me." T. W. answered that he had not wanted to intrude, that Billy would represent the whole team, and that they all were praying for the president's recovery. The president replied, "Sit down over there. I have no secrets."[2]

John F. Kennedy

T. W. Wilson spoke about an incident with President John F. Kennedy: "It was after the Presidential Prayer Breakfast, and I walked out with Billy and the president, and he got in that presidential limousine, and I heard what he said to Billy. He told him he would sure like to visit with him, but Billy said, 'Mr. President, I just can't do it; it wouldn't be fair to you, because I think I've got the flu or something.' Billy was sick, he was running a fever, and so the President said, 'I understand, but we'll do this another time.'

"We went straight back to the hotel. LBJ—he was vice president—called Billy at the hotel. He said, 'Billy, I need to talk to you.' Billy said, 'I just can't; I'm sick. I'm honored, but I'll be there as soon as I can.' I said, 'Billy, that's something that you turned them down. I bet that has never happened, that a preacher turned down the president and the vice president in the same day.'"

In his book *From a Prophet with Honor*, William Martin shares this historic moment in which T. W. Wilson was involved:

> A few days later, after President Kennedy had decided to go to Dallas (Billy Graham had an uneasiness about the trip and had tried to convey that to Kennedy), while playing golf with T. W. Wilson at a club near Montreat, Graham received word that the President and Governor Connally had been shot. They sped to a nearby BGEA-owned radio station, where Graham went on the air while Wilson called Parkland Hospital in Dallas. By a fluke of timing, they learned Kennedy was dead before the national media released the news. Graham recalls that he withheld confirmation of the death until the major networks announced it. Wilson remembers holding a scribbled note to the glass on the booth where Graham was speaking and believes the evangelist may in fact have been the first to tell a public audience, however small, that the nation had lost its leader.[3]

Richard M. Nixon

T. W. Wilson followed the 1968 presidential election closely. As it turned out, he was an astute political analyst. He recalled, "I told Billy, 'I guarantee you, Nixon's going to whip him.' Billy said, 'It sure doesn't look that way to me.' I said, 'I bet ya.'

"We walked over there from our hotel. We were going to see, hopefully, the [next] president. So Billy told Nixon, 'T. W.'s got it all figured out. He said that there's no doubt, he knows that you're going to be the next president.' Nixon said, 'How'd you figure this out? I hope you're right.' I showed him, state by state, how I'd figured it out, and he said, 'I sure hope you're right. If you are, I'm going to do something special for you.' That's how we became good friends. [By the way, T. W. was right on target.] We visited him in his homes in San Clemente and Key Biscayne, Florida, several times."

T. W. also played a part in developing what would become President Nixon's trademark gesture. Billy, T. W., and Mr. Nixon were eating at the Ocean Grill. Nixon asked T. W. and Billy if he should have some kind of trademark. Mentioning that Churchill had his own trademark, T. W. said, "I told Billy something. You may think it's kind of corny, but you're looking for some little something that people can remember you by. I saw you do something that I believe will be contagious." Nixon said, "What's that?" T. W. said, "You did like that . . . [making the V sign with both hands up]." And Nixon said, "Huh . . . Billy, what do you think about that?" And Billy said, "I think he's got a point there."

That day, when Nixon got on the plane to leave, he stood at the top of the steps, making the V sign with both hands up. T. W. recalled, "I didn't want any credit for it; he just asked me. And it impressed me for him to do that."

George Herbert Walker Bush

T. W. and President George Herbert Walker Bush developed a great friendship over the years. The Wilson family has a photo of T. W. with Mr. Bush and an elderly yet spry-looking lady. That lady was President Bush's mother, and the photo was taken during a visit to Kennebunkport.

President Bush invited T. W. to go out on a boat with him to look for porpoises. Billy didn't go, and he sat and chatted with Mrs. Bush.

During that visit, while T. W. sat in the front room with Billy and Ruth, George Bush knocked on the door, and said, "T, can I borrow you for a minute?" T. W. said, "Of course, Mr. President." He said, "Mother wants a picture of you and me together."

T. W. remembered, "You know, the thing that I liked about him so much was when we'd go around and the neighbors would say, 'Hi, George!' not 'Mr. President.'"

Reflecting on Mr. Bush's interest in the things of God and his own relationship with God, T. W. said, "President Bush was one of the best boosters. In the last crusade in Tampa, before I had my stroke, Billy had asked President Bush to come and make a speech. The president gave his testimony. It was clear-cut."

After T. W.'s death, Mary Helen received volumes of letters, cards, and calls. Two notes were from some of T. W. and Mary Helen's most admired friends:

Dear Mary Helen,

I hope you know how much Barbara and I love T. W. He was our friend and we thought the world of him. Now he is in heaven with the Lord whom he served so well.

We Bushes send you our most sincere, heartfelt condolences. We will remember forever the joy of having your wonderful husband with us on several occasions at our home in Kennebunkport.

You have, dear Mary, our family's love and our lasting respects.

Sincerely,

George Bush[4]

Another letter, handwritten, came to Mary Helen from Barbara Bush:

Dear Mrs. Wilson:

Just a note to tell you how sorry we were to hear that your precious husband, T. W., passed away. He was such a warm, marvelous man. We send you our love and to all T. W.'s family.

Warmly,

Barbara Bush[5]

George W. Bush

Another visit at the Bushes' home in Kennebunkport showed the elder Bush's spiritual concern for his family and its impact on his son, George W. Bush. T. W. recounts: "We were invited to go to their Kennebunkport, Maine, home. I remember the President said, 'Billy, you know some of my friends have been telling me about being "born again," and what is your impression about being "born again"?' Well, that just gave Billy an opportunity so he started in on what the Bible teaches about being 'born again.'

"George W. Bush, the President now, was sitting on the other side of his sister Dorothy and I was looking straight at him, and boy, he was taking it all in. Now, when he talked recently, about Billy and the feelings he had had, as far as we know, he didn't make a decision that night, but that was the renewal of his spiritual quest."

A subsequent walk on a Maine beach with Mr. Graham evidenced George W. Bush's deep interest in the things of God. He has often referred to that time as a turning point in his walk with God.

In November of 2000, during the Billy Graham Crusade in Jacksonville, Florida, T. W. had to be hospitalized in the Mayo Clinic. It was only a few days before the presidential election. During his stay at the clinic, he received a kind and encouraging note from George W. Bush. T. W. meant so much to him that during one of the most turbulent campaigns in memory, he took the time to express his concern for his friend.

Mary Helen read this letter from George H. W. Bush written to T. W. in January of 2001:

Dear T. W.,

Your wonderfully thoughtful letter just came across my desk, and I'm writing to say, "Thank you." I had not known about your condition, but am so glad that your spirits remain high.

It is certainly no secret that we Bushes have an unparalleled affection for Billy and know first-hand of his appreciation for your years of dedication to him. Kind words mean a lot to me these days, T. W., and yours were sure appreciated. George, especially, feels so fortunate to have Rev. Graham as a friend and pastor.

All the best, your friend,
George[6]

The Power of Divine Appointments

Although God may not put you in a position to influence presidents, you can be a next-level influencer. As you pray for God to use you, realize that next-level influence most often occurs in the everyday, ordinary, routine days of your life. Without fanfare, with no pomp and circumstance playing, God brings opportunities for us to affect the lives of others. "Immortality lies not in the things you leave behind, but in the people your life has touched."[7] Consider the following lessons on next-level influence.

1. Always Be Yourself

There is something really attractive about a person of authenticity and transparency. Jesus Christ was the greatest example of realness. When we take the personality God gives us and commit it to him, our uniqueness is allowed to shine through. In a world that detests anything that reeks of phoniness, being real creates quite a magnet.

T. W. Wilson was always the same person. He never tried to impress anyone or pretend to be something he was not. His humble and friendly spirit drew people to him. To the degree you allow God to influence you, you can influence others. Alan C. Emery Jr., Billy Graham Evangelistic Association board member emeritus, said of T. W., "He was always available, and he was always wanting to tell people about Jesus. He had a marvelous sense of humor—everyone wanted to be with him because he was so much fun. He would be just as nice to a hotel employee or a reporter as he would be to one of the people on the crusade program. The reason is that he saw people as the objects of the infinite love of God, and there is no distinction of persons in that."[8]

2. When God Presents an Opportunity, Take It or It Will Be Lost

When God gives you the occasion, speak up for him, because that occasion may never present itself again. Sometimes those lost opportunities have eternal consequences. When those windows of opportunity open, they may be open for only a short time.

With an open window, we can say something or do something that can leave a lasting impact upon someone. Recently I had the opportunity to lead the invocation at the chamber of commerce banquet in Lakeland, Florida. The guest speaker was Arthur O. Sulzberger Jr., publisher of the *New York Times*.

That afternoon before the banquet, I felt led by the Lord to purchase the anniversary edition of C. S. Lewis's book *Mere Christianity* and give it to our speaker. Mr. Sulzberger thanked me graciously for the book. Will he read it? Will it change his life? I don't know, but it was one window of opportunity to express the love of Christ in a tangible way.

3. Prominent People Have Great Spiritual Needs

We should not make the mistake of thinking that prominent people don't have great spiritual needs. In fact, those in authority or those who have some kind of position of influence are often searching for something more than what they have experienced. Solomon, who had it all but whose heart had become distanced from God, declared, "Then I became great and increased more than all who preceded me in Jerusalem. My wisdom also stood by me. All that my eyes desired I did not refuse them. I did not withhold my heart from any pleasure, for my heart was pleased because of all my labor and this was my reward for all my labor. Thus I considered all my activities which my hands had done and the labor which I had exerted, and behold all was vanity and striving after the wind and there was no profit under the sun" (Eccles. 2:9–11).

Solomon was looking for something beyond the realm of the five senses, beyond wealth, beyond pleasure, and beyond religion. He needed what only God could offer him. He was saying, "There has to be more to life than this." We often see this with politicians, sports celebrities, movie stars, musicians, and the wealthy. When those kinds of people see someone who genuinely lives what he believes, they often become curious and interested.

Sometimes when people possess all the trappings of success, we falsely assume that they are not interested in spiritual things. That is a dangerous assumption. T. W. noted that many "well known" people with whom he came in contact were spiritually searching. To the outside world it appeared they had it all, but that God-shaped vacuum kept them looking for something more than what they had experienced. This included not only celebrities and dignitaries but renowned criminals too. At one crusade Billy Graham was told an alleged crime boss was in the crowd. He told T. W. to go and sit with him to let him know of their love and concern for him. These men knew how to seize the moment.

4. Pray Daily for Influencers

Next-level influencers make it a matter of commitment to pray for influencers and for opportunities to influence them for Christ. Pray for these influencers' salvation. Pray that God would surround them with people of faith. Even pray for opportunities to pray personally with them.

Those in places of influence for the most part welcome our prayers. Most feel the pressure of their position and are aware they need something beyond themselves to help them. Write a note to let them know you have prayed for them.

President Lyndon Baines Johnson was a man of faith. Many could argue about his choice of words at times and even disagree with some of his decisions, but he confessed faith in Jesus Christ. On one occasion when T. W. was along with Billy Graham on a visit to the White House, they were summoned to President Johnson's bedroom. It was relatively early in the morning, and Mr. Johnson was lying on his bed in his pajamas with newspapers from major cities surrounding him. After a time of visiting, Billy asked if he could pray for the president.

T. W. recalled, "The president of the United States immediately jumped out of bed and knelt beside it. He commented, 'I will not approach my Lord and Savior Jesus Christ without being on my knees before him.'"

5. When You Influence an Influencer, You Influence Many

If you influence people of influence, you are multiplying your influence. When you affect a person who affects a lot of people, things can change quickly. President George W. Bush's faith is vital to him, and he is very public about it. He influences the world through his decisions. But think back to that meeting in Kennebunkport, Maine, when the senior George Bush asked Billy to share how a person could be born again. That meeting, which George W. Bush describes as the beginning of his spiritual journey, has now affected millions.

The next-level influencer sees that the greatest way to touch the world is strategizing to affect people in positions of influence. This is not to imply that we should ignore others. However, sometimes we neglect those in positions of influence because we feel intimidated or fearful that they will not accept what we say. Some famous people may have missed out on hearing the gospel because someone assumed they were not open to it.

6. Don't Be Afraid to Talk with People about the Bible

People are interested in the Bible—what it says, what it teaches, and how it applies to their lives. Mel Gibson's *The Passion of the Christ* started the entire country talking about Jesus and the Bible. The movie demonstrated that people are significantly interested in Christ. One challenge we should make to people in positions of prominence is to encourage them to read through the Bible, the world's all-time best-seller, in a year.

Be ready for opportunities to discuss the Bible and give answers to people's questions. That means we must study the Bible for ourselves and be ready when the opportunity emerges. "Sanctify Christ as Lord in your hearts, always being ready to make a defense to everyone who asks you to give an account for the hope that is in you, yet with gentleness and reverence" (1 Peter 3:15).

There is a great hunger in our society to know about God's Word. The fact that Rick Warren's book *The Purpose-Driven Life* has been on the *New York Times* best-seller list for so long and is the fastest selling nonfiction book in history indicates the spiritual hunger many people possess. Next-level influencers are ready to seize the moment. We not only pray for opportunities to approach people in places of influence, we proactively do whatever we can to be in their path.

5

BELOVED BARNABAS

Next-Level Influencers Are Encouragers

T. W. Wilson's sweet and encouraging spirit reflected a man who was so secure in his Lord's love that he did not need to try to impress others. Dr. Stephen Olford said he would title a book about T. W. Wilson *Beloved Barnabas* because T. W. was such an encourager to everyone in any situation. He reminded people of the encourager par excellence of the New Testament, Barnabas.

The apostle Paul would not have had his world-touching ministry had it not been for Barnabas's constant encouragement. T. W. did the same for Billy Graham. Dr. Olford spoke of times when Billy was tired, not feeling well, or just emotionally drained. T. W. pulled him out of it. He was a man who signed all of his letters, "Your Sincere Friend," and he meant it. He said, "I'd rather have a million friends than a million dollars, because every friend ought to be worth at least a dollar." T. W. had a unique ability to say no in such a way that it left people feeling encouraged and not offended. He worked at affirming other people. No wonder everyone flocked around him.

A friend of T. W., Homer Burgin, said of him, "He's the only man I know who can step on your shoes and not mess up your shoeshine." T. W. possessed the ability to encourage not only those who were prominent but everyone he met. The lives of countless unnamed prisoners, preachers, and young men and women could have been ruined had it not been for T. W.'s wise counsel setting them on the right path. (Through my many interviews with T. W., he related specific instances, but because of confidentiality, I will not share the names.) He possessed no agenda other than simply caring about people. Dr. Billy Kim describes T. W.: "I think everybody who meets him, whether they are down or discouraged, after meeting T. W. they have to be up on cloud nine. Whether they know who he is or whether they know the notoriety that he has, still, he makes everybody feel good. He makes everybody feel important."

Encouragers have influence; great encouragers have next-level influence. Betty Drummond, wife of the late Dr. Lewis Drummond, said of T. W., "He's so encouraging. He would make you think you could do more than you ever could, which makes you accomplish more." Robert Coleman, retired director of the Billy Graham Center at Wheaton College and close friend of T. W., said, "He exudes the sweetness of the Lord. T is a role model for graciousness."

T. W.'s smile was contagious. The twinkle in his eye combined with loving facial expressions encouraged people before he even said one word.

One episode took place after Billy Graham had given the invitation at a crusade. T. W. was helping counsel those who had come forward. T. W.'s encouraging persona even communicated with someone who spoke a different language. He told me, "I remember this one fellow, he couldn't speak one word of English, and of course I didn't know his language either. He came forward, and I was trying to help him, and he couldn't understand me and I couldn't understand him. I noticed something in his pocket that looked like a small Bible to me. It was a Spanish New Testament. I sent somebody to try to find somebody who could speak some Spanish. I started flipping through his New Testament, and I saw this: 'Juan.' The numerical value was the same. It was John 3:16. I started pointing to it and I said, 'Read it.' He said, '*Mi saber*' [which means "I understand that."]. I said, 'Lord, what am I going to do?' I told him, 'Repeat, repeat, repeat.' And so he began saying, '*Mi saber, Mi saber, Mi saber.*'

"Dr. Raymond Edmond, the president of Wheaton College at the time, had been a missionary and spoke Spanish. He came over and talked to him and prayed with him. Then he came over to me, and he said, 'T. W., this man has already accepted Jesus. Tell me, what did you tell him?'" T. W.'s loving approach spoke a language that this man understood.

George Beverly (Bev) Shea's wife, Karlene, worked fourteen years with T. W. in the Montreat office. This was before she married Bev. She said, "One of my favorite memories of being in the office is after a crusade. We had devotions every morning at 11:00. When it was my turn to lead the devotional, I would always ask T. W. to do it, especially after a crusade, because it was still fresh on his mind. He would bring these marvelous stories of what went on behind the scenes at the crusade, but they were stories to encourage us. You felt like you were there, and that your work was not in vain."

T. W.'s personal assistant for over thirty years, Evelyn Freeland, observed, "T. W. was one of the most gracious people that I know, and almost before he hit the office, he was writing thank-you letters. He never missed when he came back from anyplace writing thank-you letters, often on behalf of himself and Mr. Graham."

Those notes were for anyone who had done anything to assist them during a trip or crusade. T. W. even wrote thank-you notes to people who wrote him thank-you notes. His encouragement was far-reaching. This incident with the late country music legend Johnny Cash shows the power of encouragement: "We stopped to see Johnny. He was having physical problems which necessitated his constant use of oxygen. We had lunch with them. He pulled up his chair close to mine and said, 'T, you don't know what an honor it is to have you visit me.' I said, 'Oh, my word, you know Billy and Ruth just think of you and June as a brother and sister.' He said, 'But I want you to know that you have been a real friend.'"

This letter from Johnny Cash tells how T's encouragement made a difference in his life:

Dear T. W.,

The Lord is merciful. I am up and around, back in Tennessee. I am enjoying the beautiful spring weather. T. W., the letters that you've written to me over the years are precious to me. Your kindness knows no bounds. I often see Christ in you very clearly.

The Billy Graham crusades really work because of people like you who support him and have stood behind him. My love and prayers to you and everybody at your house.

Your Friend,
Johnny Cash[1]

"I Need to See Billy Graham!"

Can you imagine the number of people who have said "I need to see Billy Graham"? If everyone who wanted to see Mr. Graham saw him, he would have no time to study, pray, and prepare for his crusades. It was T. W. Wilson's task to be Graham's gatekeeper. Friend Millie Dienart said of T. W.: "Everyone wanted to see Billy Graham, and they would say, 'I'll just go to T.'" That became the standard answer to anyone wanting an appointment with Billy Graham: go to T. He was known for his graciousness.

Dr. Roger James, the late physician to both T. W. and Billy, said: "T. W. determined who needed to see Billy and who didn't, but T. W. had a knack for telling people no, and they would accept it. He did it in such a gracious way, they almost thanked him. They would come in very anxious to see Billy, and he would basically say, 'Well, that's not possible,' but they would go away almost thanking him for considering it."

Evangelist Luis Palau said: "I've seen a lot of people come up and try to see Billy Graham, and obviously he can't see them, especially in crusades because he's busy. And you know, T. W. would sit the young fellow down and say, 'What do you want to talk to him about?' And he would give him a lot of information that directly comes from Billy Graham, and the guy would walk away fulfilled, like he had talked to Billy personally. He was always positive with people. He always blessed you, always encouraged you; he never got negative."

The Tailgate of the Procession

T. W. Wilson was the follow-through guy for Billy Graham. He made sure no one who had a legitimate need to get information to Mr. Graham fell through the cracks of "too busy." Had T. W. not done that, it would have reflected negatively on Mr. Graham. He knew that, and he had an almost obsessive passion to make Billy Graham look good to the world.

Ross Rhoads, vice president of Samaritan's Purse and long-time friend, makes this point poignantly: "T. W. was the tailgate of the procession, encircling the crowd. The crowd would give, of course, a great deal of attention to Mr. Graham. T. W. would be on the side making sure that people who would like to see Mr. Graham were not overlooked or offended. He would tell people who wanted to see Mr. Graham that it was impossible but that he assured them the evangelist would do what he could. He would follow that up with a note to the person saying, 'I'm sorry you were not able to see Mr. Graham, but I conveyed the message to him.' You know, he kind of 'held court' for those who were not able to get close. He would make sure that Billy had the contact point, and if Billy was able to do it, he would then connect, and if there was a disconnect, he would compensate for the disconnect."

T. W.'s encouraging spirit not only upheld Mr. Graham's reputation but further demonstrated that one in such a position can handle people without destroying their spirit or their opinion of a person. People didn't feel they had been simply placated when T. W. explained to them that although it was not possible to see Mr. Graham, he would pass the word along to him. People felt heard, noticed, and valued when they left him.

Glenn Wilcox, one of T. W.'s closest friends and the owner of Wilcox World Travel in Asheville, North Carolina, asked T. W.

about a friend of his who wanted to remove any doubts about his salvation. They were traveling at the time, and T. W. pulled over to talk with Glenn, suspecting that it was Glenn himself and not a friend who was the object of concern. Sure enough, Glenn nailed down his salvation.

Years later when one of Glenn's sons was getting married, he asked T. W. to perform the ceremony. When T asked the groom about his salvation, he said, "Do you remember when my dad was in your car and he prayed the sinner's prayer?" T. W. said, "Of course, I will never forget that." The groom then said, "As a little boy, I was in the backseat, and when my dad prayed that prayer, I prayed it too." That is next-level influence, not only from T. W. but from a dad to his son.

Theologian Dr. John R. W. Stott said this of T. W.: "I've always admired the way in which he stood between Billy and the . . . public. Thousands of people wanted to see Billy, but they were filtered through T. W. T. W. had the gift of saying no without offending people. He had to stop many people from seeing Billy; he had to be able to say no even when they said, 'Oh, but we've come hundreds of miles to see him.' He was a diplomat in being able to shield Billy Graham from too many callers."

George Beverly Shea said of T. W.: "The human touch between the Wilsons and the Sheas was precious to me. He lived eight hundred or nine hundred feet from us, on the same street. He'd drive past our back door and just blow the horn. I liked that. We'd go to the door and he'd have a little word of encouragement: 'How are you today? What song do you have in your heart?' He was so human, yet so spiritually minded. His heart was full of love for the Lord Jesus."

Encouraging a Furniture Giant

Glenn Wilcox shared this story concerning furniture giant Ed Broyhill, who was struggling with the assurance of his salvation:

"[I approached T. W. and said,] 'T. W., I have done all I can do. Will you go with me to talk to Mr. Broyhill? He's in his late eighties or nineties, and he is worried about this, but I'm convinced beyond a shadow of a doubt that he is saved. I can't convince him of it.' He said, 'Oh, I'll be glad to.'

"So I called Mr. Broyhill, and I said, 'Mr. Broyhill, you've met T. W.; you've played golf with him. He and I would like to come down and chat with you because we really want to talk with you about your eternal salvation.' He said, 'Oh, that would be wonderful.' So we met him down in Lenoir [North Carolina], went to the office, and T. W., in the most gracious and wonderful way, walked him through the plan of salvation.

"[T. W. said,] 'Mr. Broyhill, you can make sure right now. God says, "If you will . . . I will . . ." and God's not a liar.' Mr. Broyhill said, 'Well, I didn't say he was . . .' And T. W. said, 'You can rest assured and make sure right now.' And he prayed the prayer again, and when he finished, he said, 'Whew, I feel a lot better.'

"About that time Satie Broyhill, his wife, came in, and he said, 'Satie, come over here; you need to hear what they said.' Well, she had no doubt in her mind that she was saved and going to heaven."

Encouraging Billy

Outside of his own family, T. W.'s greatest use of his powerful encouragement was with his friend Billy Graham. During crusades T. W. would always sit right behind the evangelist. It spoke volumes about T's commitment to be there for Mr. Graham. He knew Billy so well that he was always aware of those times when his friend was discouraged or needed an extra, "Billy, it's going to be all right." Often the evangelist would be physically and emotionally drained and need that trusted person who could say the right thing at the right time or just be there with him, not necessarily saying anything.

Ruth Graham knew that better than anyone. Mary Helen Wilson said, "Billy spoke at the Royal Chapel in England. . . . We were invited over to the Queen Mother's for coffee afterwards, and Prince Phillip, who got attached to T and me somehow, kept talking and talking. He said, 'Just what is your position with Dr. Graham?' T laughingly said, 'Well, Ruth calls me her "step-husband" and sometimes her "husband-in-law."' So Prince Phillip went back to Ruth later and said, 'Tell me about your step-husband. I have just been talking to him.'"

Ruth understood that T. W. often spent more time with Billy than she did when he was traveling. It became T. W.'s role to be that encourager in his life. It may have been an encouraging word, a pat on the back, an arm around his shoulder, a "You preached a great sermon tonight," a "Billy, don't worry about it; I'll take care of it," or simply a listening ear. T. W. Wilson knew how and when to encourage Billy. Ruth Graham could not have been more grateful. Neither could Billy.

The Power of Encouragement

Next-level influencers are encouragers. The world is searching for those who will take the time to encourage, something that happens less frequently in our increasingly busy society.

Encouragers lose themselves in encouraging others; they find great joy and satisfaction personally. Encouragement or edification is a gift of the Holy Spirit, but it is also a learned behavior that anyone can develop.

Doug Fields says a litmus test to determine if one needs encouragement is, "If the person is breathing, he needs encouragement."[2] Creating an atmosphere of encouragement begins with a choice. It has little if anything to do with feelings. Encouragers practice what God commanded: "Rejoice with those who rejoice, and weep with those who weep" (Rom. 12:15).

Anyone who commits to make encouraging others a way of life will become an influencer. People are drawn to those from whom they know a kind word, a positive response, and a cheerful disposition can be expected.

This is certainly seen in children. "A study was done by psychologist Dr. Henry H. Goddard on energy levels in children. He used an instrument he called the ergograph. His findings are fascinating. He found that when tired children are given a word of praise or encouragement, the ergograph shows an immediate upward surge of new energy. When the children are criticized and discouraged, the ergograph shows their physical energy takes a sudden nosedive. Those results could probably be duplicated in adults. When we are praised, our energy levels go up. When we are criticized, our energy levels go down."[3] Encouragement is powerful. Consider the following lessons on next-level influence.

1. Be a Little Kinder Than Is Necessary

Cold and nonresponsive people won't have a next-level influence. Warmth influences. A friendly person is a likeable person.

This person usually smiles and is approachable. Steve Sjogren wrote, "In medieval times there was thought to be a fearful creature dwelling in caves and crevices called a 'basilisk.' It could kill people with just one look. Of course, we no longer believe such things, and so our expression is 'if looks could kill.' Looks cannot kill, but they can often wound. Looks can also heal, encourage, and comfort."[4] Mother Teresa said, "Be kind and merciful. Let no one ever come to you without leaving better and happier. Be the living expression of God's kindness—kindness in your face, kindness in your eyes, kindness in your smile, kindness in your warm greeting."[5]

Carol Anne Hanks, T. W.'s niece, related a story that showed his kindness: "I had never been to a [Billy Graham] crusade in my life without Uncle T or Uncle Grady. Well, it makes a difference to go to a crusade with one of them. . . . Uncle Grady was already in heaven, and Uncle T was called away at the last minute. There was a fairly new staff member who didn't know me from Adam. He treated me with disrespect and rudeness. I think in an organization like this, everybody should be treated with love and kindness. But I wasn't. And my response would have been to say, 'You just shouldn't do that.'

"Uncle T asked me later, 'Well, did everything go okay? I'm sorry I couldn't be there. Was everything fine?' I said, 'Yes, basically, but . . .' I then related to him the unpleasant event. Instead of saying, 'You did wrong to this person, you shouldn't treat anybody unkindly,' or anything like that, Uncle T wrote a letter that said, 'I want to thank you for the kindness you showed to my niece, who is like my own daughter . . . and I want to tell you how grateful I am, because I couldn't be there to look after her myself.'

"That taught me a great lesson in how to respond with kindness no matter what. By the way, that person is now one of the nicest people of the whole Billy Graham team."

T. W. practiced the principle "treat people the way you want people to treat your family." He modeled what Paul admonished the Christians in Thessalonica to do: "Rejoice always; pray without ceasing; in everything give thanks; for this is God's will for you in Christ Jesus" (1 Thess. 5:16–18). Any Christian who exemplifies those three qualities will become a next-level encourager.

2. Genuinely Care about People

The world is always on the lookout for a sympathetic ear, a caring heart, and a kind face. Next-level influencers express concern for people. They don't come with answers to every problem, but they are committed to "being there" and expressing God's love. When people leave you, they need to feel they have genuinely met the compassion of Jesus Christ. Peter tells us to be "sympathetic, brotherly, kindhearted, and humble in spirit" (1 Peter 3:8).

For our task of influence, we look for opportunities to care for people. At times God presents us a small window of opportunity in a person's life when he or she is hurting and we can do something to say, "I care about you." The next-level influencer understands that everyone is either coming out of a storm, in the midst of a storm, or heading into a storm.

Stephen Covey tells of an unusual experience on a New York subway. While people were sitting quietly in the car, a man entered with his noisy and rambunctious children. The man sat down and closed his eyes as though he was oblivious to his rowdy children. The once quiet subway car was now a place of disturbing chaos.

The children's inappropriate behavior was obvious to everyone except their father.

Finally Covey confronted the man about his children. The man opened his eyes and evaluated the situation as if he were unaware of all that had transpired. Then he said, "Oh, you're right. I guess I should do something about it. We just came from the hospital, where their mother died about an hour ago. I don't know what to think, and I guess they don't know how to handle it either."[6]

Being sensitive to what people are going through at any given moment is also displayed by the prophet Ezekiel: "I sat where they sat and remained there among them seven days, overwhelmed with astonishment and silent" (Ezek. 3:15 AMP).

3. Learn to Say No without Being Offensive

Next-level influencers handle difficult situations without being offensive. They are sensitive to people's feelings. We know, however, that at times our actions and words may be taken as an offense no matter how sensitive we attempt to be. Our "no's" need to be understood not as a rejection of a person but as not being able to accommodate the request at the moment. Then the person still feels affirmed because you are not rejecting the person.

T. W. Wilson perfected this art. People left him feeling they were important, even if he had just turned down their request to speak to Mr. Graham. Next-level influencers drop their defensiveness and genuinely respond to people with love even in saying no.

4. Refuse to Be Negative

Negative people are not next-level influencers. To be a next-level influencer, one must develop a positive and proactive attitude. It is a choice and a learned trait. As Victor Frankl said, "Everything can be taken away from a man but one thing: the last of the human freedoms—to choose one's attitude in any given set of circumstances."[7]

Next-level influence is believing there are solutions to every problem, provisions for every need, answers to every issue, and resolutions to every conflict. It's the attitude that nothing is beyond the power of God to solve. This attitude is apparent in the next-level influencer's conversations. "Attitude is the mind's paintbrush, it can color any situation."[8] With the right kind of attitude, you will be known as an encourager.

Not being negative becomes a choice we must constantly make. This is not a Pollyanna approach to life but one that simply believes the best and lives in the reality that God is in control. Like the second law of thermodynamics, a positive attitude will tend to become negative unless there is an outside intervention. That outside intervention for the Christian is a daily time of encountering God on bended knee with an open Bible.

Winston Churchill said, "I have no secret. You haven't learned life's lesson very well if you haven't noticed that you can give the tone or color, or decide the reaction you want of people in advance. It's unbelievably simple. If you want them to smile, smile first. If you want them to take an interest in you, take an interest in them first. If you want to make them nervous, become nervous yourself. If you want them to shout and raise their voices, raise yours and shout. If you want them to strike you, strike first. It's as simple as that. People will treat you like you treat them. It's no secret. Look about you. You can prove it with the next person you meet."[9] Next-level influencers determine to be positive based on faith in God.

5. Encouragement Has Many Expressions

Encouragement has many forms, yet the effect is virtually always the same—influence. Legendary UCLA basketball coach John Wooden had a special way of making sure his players encouraged each other. Wooden instructed his players that whenever a basket was made, the scoring player was required to smile, wink, or nod at the player who passed him the ball. When Coach Wooden gave these instructions to the team, one new player asked, "But coach, what if he's not looking?" Wooden replied, "I guarantee he'll look."[10]

Henry Ford once said that the ability to encourage others is one of life's finest assets. The auto inventor and manufacturer knew the power of encouragement. He learned it as a young man. Young Ford had endured criticism and ridicule for his newly built engine. Most mechanical experts of that day were convinced that electric carriages would be the popular passenger cars of the future.

Ford attended a dinner one evening at which Thomas Edison was present. Ford began explaining his engine to the ones nearest him at a table. He noticed that Edison, seated several chairs away, was listening. Finally the great man moved closer and asked the young inventor to make a drawing. When the crude sketch was complete, Edison studied it intently, then suddenly banged his fist on the table. "Young man," he said, "that's the thing! You have it!" Years later, Ford recalled, "The thump of that fist upon the table was worth worlds to me."[11]

People everywhere are looking for a little encouragement. T. W. Wilson demonstrated that encouragement is a way of life, not a onetime act or word. For every occasion there is an appropriate form of encouragement. Sometimes it means just your presence with people—sitting with them, weeping with them, or remaining silent together with them. Encouragement may be a hug, a pat on the back, a high five, or a tap on the shoulder. At other times it may be a card, a note, a letter, or an email that expresses concern. Encouragement may take the form of a compliment or a piece of constructive criticism ever-so-carefully offered. The next-level influencer constantly thinks about how to encourage others.

6

CLOSE CALLS

Next-Level Influencers Trust God

T. W. Wilson knew firsthand the protection of God. There were many instances where just one minute sooner, one minute later, or one step closer could have brought disastrous results.

Mr. Graham cannot imagine anyone desiring to harm him, but those around him understand the risks. That is a credit to T. W., who rarely let Billy know about the threats. T. W. Wilson's towering physique and disarming firmness more than once prevented harm from coming upon Billy. Although T. W. wouldn't want it said this way, he was Billy's bodyguard. He was alert to everything going on around them. There was no time to blink.

T. W. recounted several dangerous situations he encountered while with the Graham team: "I remember once when we were in Sweden, Cliff Barrows, Bev Shea, and I were sitting on the front row while Billy was speaking.

"There was a person sitting right next to me, and here I was supposed to be making sure that no one harmed Billy. Billy told something humorous, and we were all looking at him and laughing with no notice of this woman, who had something in her purse that we were unaware of. She went up and threw acid on Billy. Fortunately, it didn't hurt him, but it did ruin his clothes.

"I remember another occasion in one of the American crusades. There were five different people who had come into the stadium with arms—pistols—who were planning to assassinate Billy Graham. The ushers and team members caught three of them and got them out . . . but there were two others who stayed inside. Their plan didn't work, but it was a very close call."

T. W. gave another incident: "There was an occasion in one of the European crusades that happened five minutes before Billy was finished (actually during the invitation). I got a call on my two-way radio that I should take Billy out a different route because where he normally went out to the automobile there were some problems. I didn't know what they were except that my job was to get him out a different way. Grady was on the platform, and I told him to go out and get the car and bring it down as close as he could to third base.

"So when we left the platform, I told Billy that we were going a different way. He said, 'What's up?' I said, 'I'll tell you later.' So we walked to third base in the stadium and found the security people with Grady and the car waiting to take us back to the hotel. We learned later in the police report that there were two people (unknown to each other) at his normal exit location. They both had one thing in mind—they wanted to kill Billy Graham.

One of them had a pistol and the other had an awful-looking knife. Anyway, the security people were on the alert, and they arrested both of them."

Don Tabb, who oversaw the counseling and follow-up ministry for the Billy Graham Evangelistic Association from 1966 to 1972, shared this close call that occurred in 1969: "Clebe McClary, the decorated war veteran, had just given his testimony. A car came onto center field, ambling in. Clebe had been delivered to the stage, because he was not ambulatory. I thought it was a car coming to pick him up. But all of a sudden it stopped about 50 yards behind the platform, and these three people jumped out, and one had a wheelchair, and though he was not crippled, he jumped in the wheelchair and this other guy begins to wheel him around, and he's shouting, 'What . . . are you going to do about this, Billy Graham?'

"It so happened that there were thirty-five security personnel that night and thirty-four of them were in the press box having coffee. There was one man on duty on the platform. So I went over there and I tackled the lead guy, and Ted Dienert hit the other one and knocked him to the ground. One of them did have a gun.

"We somehow got them all back in the car, and they pulled the keys away. We couldn't find the key and the front wheels were locked in a right-hand position, so we literally, with ten or fifteen of our counselors and ushers, pushed the car with the wheels not rolling back out, and then we turned them over to the police.

"But where T got involved was the next morning. T said, 'You know, Billy, Don really messed up his gray suit on that guy.' Billy had a wonderful supporter down there that was in the clothing business, so he told me to go to Mooney's and get a new suit. It was the most beautiful, green worsted suit you've ever seen. I was so proud of that suit. I wore it on the night of the big rain in the Baton Rouge crusade and I was completely soaked. My new suit was ruined, but Billy was safe."

T. W. tells of another occasion: "In another place, I think it was Arizona, when Billy and I got out of the car, we went in the back way and there were a number of people there to welcome us. One of the security men asked, 'T. W., what does that man over there in the gray suit do for you?' I said, 'What man?' He pointed and I said, 'I've never seen him before.' So they said to him, 'We need a word with you.'

"We learned that this man had in his mind to assassinate Billy, and he was just a foot away from him. There were several close calls like these, but actually there is no protection better than the protection of the Lord himself. In different countries, in different places, there were some undesirable people who wanted to get rid of Billy Graham. Most of them were in the United States, I'm embarrassed to say."

Concerning security issues with Billy Graham, William Martin said, "According to T. W. Wilson, the evangelist received more threats of violence during the mid-1980s than over the thirty years prior to that. Pulling out a four-inch folder filled with vile imprecations that documented his point, he said, 'We turn all threats over to the FBI, and they look into it. Some of the language is so filthy, and the hatred so bitter, you wouldn't believe it. If they really want you,' Wilson conceded, 'they can usually get you, but we take all the threats seriously. We have more trouble with religious nuts than anything else.'"[1]

"T. W. Wilson checks it out to make sure no woman is hiding in the closet or the bathroom or lurking behind the drapes. Once Mr. Graham is in the room alone, he will not answer the door unless he knows for certain who has knocked."[2] Suffice it to say that T. W. did everything humanly possible to protect Mr. Graham, but he also relied on God's supernatural hedge of protection.

A Close Call That Delivered a Life Verse

Early in his ministry, T. W. Wilson learned that God is in total control of every circumstance in his life. He said, "I remember landing at the airport in Atlanta, and I was going to make a connection to go to Charlotte, North Carolina, where my parents lived. This was in the days before the frequency of flights. I was on a little DC-3, and I felt so fortunate to get a flight. I was on the plane, my luggage was on, and this man came and said, 'Mr. Wilson?' I raised my hand and he said, 'Mr. Wilson, we'll have to ask you to get off because we have a gentleman here who has had his ticket for two weeks, and you just booked yours.'

"I grumbled and griped and said, 'What kind of an outfit are you running around here?' I went back to the terminal, a little airport at that time. I couldn't find any bus or anything. Finally they told me that there was a bus leaving for Charlotte in I forget just how many minutes, but that was when there was one road from the Atlanta airport. It had so many traffic lights on it. I caught a taxi and I said to the driver, 'There is a bus that is going to leave the bus station in a few minutes. If you'll get me there, I'll double your fare.' He said, 'It's a deal.'

"So he ran through red lights and we pulled up and I didn't have a chance to buy a ticket before I got on the bus. The first bus stop, I got out and called Daddy because I knew he would be worried about me not being on that plane.

"I called home and my dad answered. He said, 'Who is this?' I said, 'Daddy, it's T. W.' He said, 'Oh son, oh son!' I said, 'Daddy, what's the matter?' Finally he said, 'The plane that you said you were on crashed, and everybody on it was killed.'

"I stood there in that phone booth and thought of all the griping I had done. The plane had crashed. That's when I chose Romans 8:28 as my life verse: 'And we know that all things work together for good to them that love God, to them who are the called according to his purpose.'"

T. W. Wilson: Assistant U.S. Marshal

Few people realize that T. W. was an assistant U.S. Marshal. This gave him the authority to carry a firearm anywhere in the world. He said, "The way that happened—we were in Washington, and Billy had spoken at this big meeting. And then some of the executives from the meeting invited Billy, and of course I was along, but we had some problem people that night that were pretty strong, and I came to Billy's rescue.

"So, after we got straightened out and got away from that little crowd, we went into the reception. The wife of Senator Mark Hatfield, Antoinette, said, 'T. W., why doesn't he get some police officer to follow him?' I said, 'He won't fool with police officers.' She said, 'Well, Mark can get you made a U.S. Marshal.' I said, 'A U.S. Marshal?' So she motioned Mark over and talked to him, and he said, 'Why, certainly, I can arrange that.'

"I said, 'It's just that simple?' Well, I didn't know it, but they had been checking on where I went to high school and college and what kind of student [I was] and my integrity. They checked the bank and everything. About three months later I got a call from the U.S. Marshal's office, and they said, 'We'd like to have you come to the U.S. Marshal's office.' So I went to the one in Asheville, and he said, 'I've been talking to Senator Mark Hatfield, and he recommended you. Would you be willing?' I said, 'My, well, what would I have to do?' He said, 'It would give you privileges to arrest people and carry a weapon.' I said, 'My goodness, I hadn't thought about all of that.'

"Well, Billy was encouraging me to do it, and they had already talked to not only Billy but members of his family, his wife, Ruth. She related this to me, and she said, 'I wasn't so sure that I was going to recommend you (ha-ha).' Well, anyway, for five or six years, I was an assistant federal marshal."

In the federal marshal program at that time, candidates had to learn to shoot from a variety of distances and also to shoot with each hand. T. W. recalled: "Well, I had never shot a pistol in my life with my left hand. The reason for that is, you see, for instance if you are in the line of duty and you are shot in the right side, you need to be able to shoot with your left. I said, 'Oh, good night, I've never shot a gun with my left hand. I couldn't shoot a thing.' You'd be surprised.

"So with a little bit of instruction, they had me shooting a pistol with my left hand. I didn't even know how to shoot lining it up with my left eye, because I'd always used my right eye. And so they had me practicing. And what do you know, to my amazement, I got to be more proficient with my left hand than I did my right hand. Now why? Because the right hand is my stronger hand, and your tendency is to overpower, and with the left, you have to depend upon your marksmanship, in other words."

T. W. decided to resign after five or six years because marshals had to requalify every six months. With his travel schedule, it was virtually impossible to practice shooting. At his last requalification he missed a perfect score by only two points. When time came for his next requalification, he decided to resign. Because of his previous high score, they offered to let him skip the test and tried to persuade him to stay. However, T. W. had already made up his mind. He said he hated being "a sitting duck": "Oh, there was one time up on the edge of Canada, in Michigan, that was pretty rough. We had five different fellows, not together, but we'd been tipped off that they were going to try to get to Billy. I just thought, *You've got all these police officers around us. I'm a minister. Why should I be fooling around here?*"

T. W. admitted that he finally quit telling Billy about the threats and just figured he would "get up under the power of the Holy Spirit and preach and not be encumbered by the threats." T. W. said, "Billy would go around bragging, 'You know, T is an assistant federal marshal.' I'd say, 'Man, you're going to get me killed.' So he was kind of upset, not really upset, but a little bit, when I resigned. He said, 'Man, I know so many fellows who would give their right arm to be a federal marshal, and here you give it up.'"

They retired his badge, which is not usually done, and gave it to him. Fortunately, T. W. never had to use his weapon.

"Would a Prayer Be in Order, Sir?"

Obviously flying on an airplane was second nature to Billy Graham and T. W. Wilson. They flew everywhere. However, they learned to never take for granted asking God for protection every time they boarded a plane. T. W. shared this serious, yet somewhat comical instance: "We were 41,000 feet up, in a plane provided by a friend, going from Chicago to Minneapolis. Several people offered to give Billy a plane, but he always refused. The fact that friends would insist on flying Billy places became a blessing since commercial travel would have been very difficult for him. We were flying in bad weather and all of a sudden, 'BOOM!' It was just like we had hit a big something or other, and then immediately awful smoke was coming into the cabin, and of course they had a way to get rid of that, but, my, it was about to choke us.

"I'll never forget when the copilot turned around, addressed Billy, and said, 'Would a prayer be in order, sir? We've had a mechanical problem.' The weather was so bad we couldn't land. So we kept flying until we got to a city where we could land.

"We got on another plane to take us on to Minneapolis. Which shows that we weren't reflecting on the pilots. But I've had seven of those close calls."

Belfast

God protected Billy Graham and the team on trips to Belfast, Northern Ireland. T. W. said, "That was during that awful time when they were fighting each other. They had blown up a part of the hotel where we were staying, and I sent my laundry out, and Billy's. No vehicle was allowed to be parked without somebody in it in downtown Belfast. Before we could get our laundry back, the laundry was blown up. Somebody was killed in the hotel on the second floor where we had the press conference.

"On another occasion, we started to go into a restaurant but didn't. This fellow had ordered something to eat. He brought some flowers. When the lady went to get the order, he walked out, and then the bomb in the flowers went off. We had gone on to the next block and were near enough to know about this. It was awful.

"We had to take subways because you couldn't get a taxi. It was a bad thing. But let me tell you the miraculous thing that happened there: from the opening night of the crusade right on through, I think we were there five nights without one problem, not one shooting, not one anything."

Richard Bewes, Rector of All Saints' Langham Place, offered his insight into T. W.'s relationship with Billy Graham: "I've noticed that Billy Graham never goes through the door first. T. W. will say, 'After you, Billy.' And he'll say, 'Oh, no, after you.' I have wondered why, then I think, 'Oh, I know why—because he's got to be the "advance man."'" He opens the door, sees if there's any trouble there, and if there is, you back out. T. W. does that. He's the advance scout, just to make sure there is no trouble ahead.

"Once Billy was preaching, and it was a wonderful night, and afterwards Bob Williams, a team member, says to T. W., 'There's a man outside the side entrance. Just go out and make sure it is alright.' And that's what T. W. would do. He would go confront the man and say, 'Hello, I'm T. W. Wilson,' and interview him quickly. T. W. is the defuser of the public."

The Power of Trusting God

Romans 8:28 is a great life verse. The Old Testament version of that verse is Genesis 50:20: "As for you, you meant evil against me, but God meant it for good in order to bring about this present result, to preserve many people alive." Both verses teach us that God is always in control, even when it appears to us that he is not. When we embrace these verses, appearances are laid on the altar of faith. We choose to believe God no matter what.

Ronald Reagan remarked, "God has a plan and it isn't for us to understand, only to know that He has His reasons and because He is all merciful and all loving we can depend on it that there is purpose in whatever He does and it is for our own good."[3] Consider the following lessons on next-level influence.

1. Understand That Evil Is Real in the World

The next-level influencer has the conviction that God and good have an enemy called evil. This evil constantly lurks and searches for an opportunity to manifest itself. Behind evil is a real, personal enemy, not just a force of evil. His name is Satan. Where evil is present, Satan is present. The source of evil is not fate, bad luck, or a certain alignment of the stars.

Next-level influencers see evil for what it is and believe that evil is not the most powerful force in the world. With that in mind we set out, in the power of a resurrected Savior, to do something about the present evil in the world. Christians are confident that anytime evil meets Christ, Christ wins.

Our confidence is in the fact that Jesus's dying on the cross was God's ultimate answer to evil in the world. With confidence in that message we possess the sincere belief that the world can change. Next-level influencers see it as their duty to follow Paul's admonition, "Do not be overcome by evil, but overcome evil with good" (Rom. 12:21).

2. Remember That Anytime You Attempt Something Great for God, You Will Face Resistance

The next-level influencer will attempt great things for God. He or she will also, however, expect resistance from the enemy. It is not a matter of *if*, it is a matter of *when* that struggle will come. Resistance is Satan's way of attempting to fill us with fear about following God's will. He hopes we will back off, let up, or give up.

Satan threatens us with *what ifs*. He throws his fiery darts at our minds, attempting to get us to doubt God. He flings his blazing missiles at our hearts, attempting to get to our emotions. He pulls the switch on his weapons aimed at our faith. And if our enemy cannot bring us down with a direct hit, he will attack someone whose wounding will distract and discourage us. The next-level influencer must be able to come to the place where he can say, like Paul, "no advantage [will] be taken of us by Satan, for we are not ignorant of his schemes" (2 Cor. 2:11). Although Satan cannot read our minds, he is aware of God's activity and will resist it.

3. Trust God's Protection, But Don't Take Any Chances

The sovereign God is in control of the universe, in control of our lives, and in control of all things. Trusting in him gives us the freedom to go where we need to go and do what we need to do as next-level influencers. However, living in the fear of what might happen can easily paralyze a person into inactivity. Fear must not be allowed that kind of influence in our lives.

John Wesley said, "My life is immortal until my work on earth is done."[4] This is not to suggest that we don't take every precaution to be safe. Anytime we travel by air, we're reminded that our world has changed since September 11, 2001. Although reassuring, beefed-up airport screenings are not what bring us our greatest sense of security. Our confidence in God alone, who called us to a task, is what brings us our greatest peace of mind. The task of becoming a next-level influencer armed with a message is impenetrable even to the best of our enemy's weapons.

4. Refuse to Allow Fear to Paralyze

Next-level influencers learn from every close call, every attack from the enemy, and every protection from disaster. These things build our faith that God is indeed in control of the circumstances of our lives. We learn to be thankful for every moment he gives us on planet earth and to never take life for granted. We further learn that fear is a fact of life but must never paralyze us from our assigned task of influencing the world in a Christ-ward direction. People who are paralyzed by what could happen to them or what others might say or think live in a fear-induced bondage.

The Billy Graham team could have easily been paralyzed by fear, never knowing when and where attacks upon Mr. Graham's life might come. But they chose, as next-level influencers, to admit their fears and then exchange them for the certainty that God makes no mistakes.

5. Prayer Does Matter

Prayer is always in order. God uses prayer to catapult us into the arena of our greatest influence. Prayer not only encourages but fills us with courage. The Scottish Reformer John Knox was not held in the highest favor by Queen Mary, who was known as Bloody Mary. One day on his way to court, he was warned that it might be better to postpone his visit as she was in an angry mood. He replied, "Why should I be afraid of a queen when I have just spent three hours with God?"[5]

Prayer influences God and impacts the outcome. Prayer changes things, but primarily prayer changes us—and when we are changed, we can produce change. T. W. Wilson and Billy Graham spent much time in prayer. Because somebody prayed, God protected the team from a bomb, an airplane in serious trouble, and multiple assassination plots on Billy Graham's life.

Next-level influencers understand that the power of their influence is in direct proportion to their commitment to prayer. David Bruce, Mr. Graham's current executive assistant, shared an incredible insight. Though Billy Graham faces many physical ailments, Bruce said, "We know that if we can get Mr. Graham to the place of the crusade, he will be infused with strength because at that moment, that is the most prayed-for place in the world." That is influential, pivotal praying.

John Hull and Tim Elmore write in their excellent book *Pivotal Praying*, "Pivotal prayers come at pivotal moments. They produce pivotal decisions and result in pivotal consequences. Pivotal praying means we pray consistently from our hearts, not just from our heads. It is birthed out of relationship, not routine. Pivotal prayers move past clichés and perfunctory phrases to meaningful exchanges with God. . . . Key moment. Key prayer. Key results."[6] Next-level influencers value this kind of prayer.

6. Take Out the Word Coincidence

The word *coincidence* means, "the occurrence of events that happen at the same time by accident but seem to have some connection."[7] Things don't "just happen" in the life of a Christian. A divine design is at work in the life of every child of God. Some say that coincidence is when God chooses to remain anonymous. Vance Havner, a close friend of T. W. Wilson and Billy Graham, said, "All my days I have been aware of One going before me and with me, of doors ajar that I never could have opened."[8] The opportunities presented to us to influence people are not chance encounters.

7

COUNSELING MR. GRAHAM

Next-Level Influencers Are Discerning

The relationship between T. W. Wilson and Billy Graham was built upon the utmost trust and love for each other. That gave T. W. the opportunity to be a counselor and friend to Billy. Billy knew that whatever T. W. told him was based upon the pure motive of desiring to do what was best for his friend. He valued T.'s advice and counsel.

The uniqueness of their relationship gave T. W. the freedom to tell Mr. Graham his honest opinion. It was that way from the beginning of their ministry together. T. W. realized that he would be no help to Billy if he didn't have the liberty to share his opinion, especially when Billy asked him for it. Billy needed honest answers and forthright opinions on issues that would affect his ministry. He needed frankness, not flattery.

In T. W. he found someone who would dare say, "I think you are wrong," "You'd better rethink that," "I don't agree with you," or "You are making a mistake." T. W. had no other agenda besides helping Billy. There was no insecurity or jealousy in his heart toward Mr. Graham.

In fact, it was just the opposite. T. W. said, "I want to say this with all sincerity: I don't have a greater hero than Billy himself. I know the real Billy Graham. I don't think he could fool me if he tried, because I have seen him and traveled with him and lived with him under all kinds of circumstances. I've seen him when his life was threatened, when people insisted they had to see him and would try any kind of trick to get into his hotel room. But I believe that Billy Graham is probably the most sincere hero that I would want to talk about."

T. W. smiled as he recalled some of those times when he would say to Billy, "Do you want me to tell you what you want to hear or tell you what I think?" During a friendly disagreement, T. W. commented to Billy, "You can believe what you want to, but you're wrong."

T. W. said, "I've never corrected him in front of anybody. I wanted to a number of times, but I didn't. Afterwards I'd say, 'Billy, by the way, you said thus and so, and I'm going to tell you why I don't agree with you.' He would say, 'Oh, you think you know everything, don't you?' And I'd say, 'No, but I know a few things, and I know that you're just dead wrong on that.'" He also added with a twinkle in his eyes, "Thank God that some of the things I told Billy Graham to do, he didn't do."

Billy Graham said of T. W., "I had years of well-founded confidence in T. W., not only as a friend but as a watchdog when I was away. T. W. has been so much a part of my life since youth that I feel as if he has been with our ministry forever. A gifted evangelist who held citywide meetings for years before joining our Team, T. W. often is a wise and practical counselor to people in trouble. His humor and his willingness to work long hours have been a source of great encouragement to all of us. I've leaned on him in practical ways perhaps more than on any other person in recent years."[1]

It's Time for My Pastor

T. W. spent many days and nights on the road and in hotels with Mr. Graham. The specific location of the hotel where Mr. Graham was staying was unknown to virtually everyone except T. W. His room would always be across the hall or adjacent to Mr. Graham's. The evangelist needed his privacy and personal time with God. It was T. W.'s responsibility to protect Billy's energy and his anointing. Everything had to revolve around him being at his best for the crusade.

T. W. recalled a scene that often took place while Mr. Graham was in his room in a crusade city. T. W. would let room service in for Mr. Graham and then let him eat his breakfast. "One of the things that meant a lot to me the last two or three years [was that] he'd call me after breakfast, and I don't think he himself knew what it meant to me, he'd call me and he'd say, 'Well, it's time for my pastor.'

"I'd take my Bible and I'd go over there and I'd say, 'Billy, do you have a special place you want me to read?' Sometimes, he'd say, 'Yeah, read so and so' and other times he'd say, 'Well, you just choose.' And so we'd read, and we'd make some comments, and I'd say, 'Billy, what do you think about this?' And he'd be lying in the bed, in pajamas, just comfortable, and once in a while he would say, 'You know, I hadn't thought of this.' He'd say to me, 'You know, T, you really amaze me!' He'd say some kind things like that."

Jim Wilson, T. W.'s son and an evangelist himself, said, "Daddy would preach to Uncle Billy, and Uncle Billy would preach to the world. Sometimes Uncle Billy would come to Daddy and say, 'You know, I need an illustration here,' and Daddy would give him one." He further related this moving story: "It's an interesting thing about Billy Graham, when Daddy had his stroke, he tried to persuade him to come back even after he had been through some therapy and gotten out of the hospital. He said, 'I need you to just come and travel with me.'

"Of course, Daddy couldn't do it. Uncle Billy said, 'Well, I'll sign us into the hotel, I'll carry the bags, I'll do this, I'll do that.' Daddy knew that would never happen. And then Uncle Billy said, 'I'll be the pastor for both of us, you know, you used to read to me, now I'll read to you.'"

Counseling for Mr. Graham

T. W. Wilson had an approachability that made people feel comfortable seeking his advice. His position as Billy Graham's executive assistant gave him an opportunity to counsel many people coming from all walks of life. He shared with me a conversation he had with a very wealthy lady. Her first husband abandoned her after she was converted in 1957 at the Billy Graham New York City crusade. Her second husband died and left her a fortune. She became a very effective soul winner. T. W. said, "One day she called me and asked if I would preach her funeral." He agreed to do so, saying, "If it will honor

T. W. Wilson at his child-
hood home in Charlotte,
North Carolina.

T. W. Wilson and Mary Helen Sellers.
Married June 26, 1942. Dothan, Alabama.

On the eve of departure to England for six months in Europe (1947–48). T. W. preached, and the Couriers for Christ Quartet sang at Youth for Christ rallies. Middle row, right to left: Mrs. T. W. Wilson Sr., Mary Helen Wilson, Jimmy Wilson, T. W. Wilson.

T. W. Wilson, Grady Wilson, Billy Graham, George Beverly Shea. Pentagon, Washington, DC. January 28, 1952.

T. W. Wilson and Billy Graham in the Montreat, North Carolina, office.

T. W., Mary Helen, Sally, and Jim Wilson (left to right). Maranatha Bible Conference, Muskegon, Michigan. Around 1955.

T. W. Wilson, Billy Graham, President and Mrs. Johnson (left to right). November 28, 1965.

T. W. Wilson, Bunny Graham, Mrs. Nixon, President Nixon (party nominee), Mrs. Mark Hatfield, Sally Wilson (left to right). Billy Graham Crusade, Pittsburgh, Pennsylvania, 1968.

T. W. Wilson, President Dwight Eisenhower, and Billy Graham (left to right) at Eisenhower's farm in Gettysburg, Pennsylvania.

T. W. Wilson at work in his office in Montreat, North Carolina, 1980.

Dr. W. A. Criswell and T. W. Wilson (left to right).

Johnny Cash and T. W. Wilson, 1981.

Billy Graham and T. W. Wilson on the crusade platform, 1984.

President and Mrs. George H. W. Bush and T. W. Wilson, 1992.

T. W. Wilson and Billy Graham on the Grahams' front porch, 1993.

T. W. Wilson at the Great Wall of China, 1994.

T. W. and Mary Helen Wilson, 2000.

T. W. Wilson's
gravestone. Mountain
View Memorial Park,
Black Mountain,
North Carolina.

"T W"
THOMAS WALTER WILSON
JUN 30 1918   MAY 24 2001
BELOVED HUSBAND
DADDY GRANDDADDY
MAN OF GOD
PREACHER OF THE GOSPEL
FAITHFUL SERVANT OF JESUS CHRIST
ROMANS 8:28

the Lord and give glory to him, I will be glad, if I'm still alive." Not long after that, she called T. W. and wanted his advice on investing a considerable amount of money to the right cause. That is just one example of how T. W. used his wisdom to steer people to an even greater impact for Christ. His counsel was never characterized by selfish motives, and people knew it. Multiple people, especially those in the ministry, have been the recipients of T. W. Wilson's gracious advice when they had the good sense to seek it.

The Great Society

Grady Wilson, T. W.'s younger brother, also had significant influence on Billy Graham until his early death.

The late Dr. Lewis Drummond gave his account of an episode during Lyndon Johnson's presidency. The president had mapped out his social plan called "the Great Society." He asked Billy Graham to head it. Billy Graham has an enormous concern for every aspect of the needs of people. Dr. Drummond told the story:

"Billy contemplated and contemplated this offer. Billy said, 'I want the world to know that I'm not concerned just about people's salvation; I want them to know I'm concerned about feeding the hungry and clothing the naked.' So he pondered it a long time, and finally T and Billy Graham were in a hotel room one day and Billy said, 'T, get the president on the phone. I'm going to accept it.'

"So T went over to pick up the telephone to call the president, and Grady walked in right at that moment. Billy said, 'Grady, I've told T to get on the telephone and call the president and tell him

I'm going to accept the position to head up the Great Society program. What do you think about it?' Now, you would have to know Grady. Grady said, 'Well, that's the first time I've ever heard God call somebody and then un-call them.' He turned around and walked out.

"That was Grady. Grady used to say of Billy Graham, 'God, you keep him strong, and I'll keep him humble.' So then Billy said, 'T, don't call the president.'"

The Statement That Never Made It to Press

T. W. Wilson was tremendously discerning in dealing with people and in dealing with the press. During the time of the fall of Jim Bakker and the controversy over his PTL ministry in Charlotte, North Carolina, the press kept putting pressure on Billy Graham to make a statement. So Billy finally wrote a statement for the press. He planned to release it the next day through the media people in Minneapolis when T. W. got a copy of the statement and decided to call a friend who worked for the *Asheville Citizen-Times*. He asked the journalist, a Christian, to evaluate how the liberal press would react to the statement.

The reporter gave T. W. a three- or four-page critique. He took it immediately to Billy and Ruth. He wanted them both to hear what the reporter had said.

When they saw the critique, Billy said to T. W., "What in the world? I didn't say that! Good night, you mean they would interpret it that way?" He hadn't even read halfway through the critique when he picked up the phone, called Minneapolis, and said, "I want you to shred that thing I gave you. Don't you dare put that out there."

The Power of Counsel

Next-level influencers have the opportunity to offer their advice. That right, however, has to be earned by exhibiting trust-worthiness, godly wisdom, a deep walk with the Lord, and a commitment to listening.

President Dwight Eisenhower described his mother as a smart and saintly lady: "Often in this job I've wished I could consult her. But she is in heaven. However, many times I have felt I knew what she would say." One night in their home on the farm, Mrs. Eisenhower was playing a card game with her boys. "Now, don't get me wrong," said the former president. "It was not with those cards that have kings, queens, jacks, and spades on them. Mother was too straitlaced for that." President Eisenhower said the game they were playing was called Flinch. "Anyway, Mother was the dealer, and she dealt me a very bad hand. I began to complain. Mother said, 'Boys, put down your cards. I want to say something, particularly to Dwight. You are in a game in your home with your mother and brothers who love you. But out in the world you will be dealt bad hands without love. Here is some advice for you boys. Take those bad hands without complaining and play them out. Ask God to help you, and you will win the important game called life.'" The president added, "I've tried to always follow that wise advice."[2]

Listening to people baring their innermost thoughts and struggles helps us to earn the right to influence them either by what we say or what we don't say. One of the skills T. W. Wilson developed was the skill of answering a question with a question. It got people talking and put him in the position of being able to insert his opinion once that person had talked so much he was ready to listen. Talk show hosts surround us, dispensing advice from a secular point of view. Next-level influencers offer counsel from a biblical worldview. Consider the following lessons on next-level influence.

1. A Person Who Can Be Trusted

The next-level influencer can be trusted to always tell you what is right, not just what you want to hear. By no means is he a "yes-man." He won't keep silent just to keep from temporarily hurting someone's feelings, although he is sensitive to those feelings. He would rather run the risk of hurting your feelings than have you make a wrong decision or go down an unwise path. He doesn't want you to hurt your credibility and, more importantly, Christ's name.

Plenty of people will tell you what you want to hear. Unfortunately, we often surround ourselves with those people because it is within our comfort zone. Initially this may prove to be exhilarating, but in the long term it can be destructive.

The next-level influencer is not a flatterer. That's why T. W. Wilson was so valuable to Billy Graham. His honesty helped prevent Mr. Graham from saying or doing some things that he might later regret. Oliver Cromwell once told the man who was painting his portrait, "Mr. Lely, I desire you would use all your skill to paint my picture truly like me, and not flatter me at all; but re-mark all these rough-nesses, pimples, warts, and everything as you see me, otherwise I will never pay a farthing for it."[3]

The next-level influencer doesn't dwell on what's wrong, but he doesn't hesitate to try to avert someone from making a great mistake. On the other hand, the person of next-level influence must be open to that same kind of admonition from others.

The next-level influencer embraces Paul's principle of "speaking the truth in love" (Eph. 4:15). When the occasion comes, he doesn't stutter concerning the truth, even in the presence of prominent people. "Righteous lips are the delight of kings, and he who speaks right is loved" (Prov. 16:13).

2. Seeks the Wisdom of God

Next-level influencers daily claim James 1:5, "But if any of you lacks wisdom, let him ask of God, who gives to all generously and without reproach, and it will be given to him." They continually seek the wisdom of God, knowing that he alone is the only source of wise advice to offer. Wisdom is knowing what to do with what you know. It is godly common sense, practical in nature and strengthened through experience. J. I. Packer calls wisdom "the practical side of moral goodness."[4] How could T. W. Wilson have helped Billy Graham unless he possessed the wisdom of God?

One of the great by-products of God's wisdom is discernment. That is what Paul prayed for the Philippians: "And this I pray, that your love may abound still more and more in real knowledge and all discernment, so that you may approve the things that are excellent" (Phil. 1:9–10). Discernment is the God-given ability to see through things, people, and circumstances and help determine the motive. Further, discernment allows one to determine if something is of God, of Satan, or simply something our flesh desires. Discernment is God's radar system, given to us as we seek his wisdom. It dares to ask questions, probing to discover the "what" and "why" of a situation. As John Maxwell rightly notes, "Smart leaders believe only half of what they hear. Discerning leaders know which half to believe."[5]

Discernment means we are not gullible or easily misled. Lyndon Johnson said, "A president's hardest task is not to do what is right, but to know what is right."[6] Discernment helps us to determine the answer to "What is the right thing?" This divine insight into issues helps us to know where and with whom we need to invest our time for maximum impact. We need the wisdom of God in order to say yes and no to the right people and things.

3. A Passionate Devotional Life

The next-level influencer finds strength from daily times spent reading and meditating on God's Word and prayer. There are no shortcuts when it comes to a disciplined devotional life. Nothing can substitute for time spent with God in order to grow spiritually; to gain strength for spiritual warfare; to put the mind, will, and emotions under the Spirit's control; and to gain insight into the will of God.

An exploring party, with the help of national guides, was forcing its way at a fast pace through the jungles. Still far from the day's agreed-upon destination, the guides sat down. "Are they sick?" the leader was asked. "No." "Are they tired?" "No." "Then why are they stopping?" The leader explained that they had a good reason. They had traveled so far and fast that it was time for them to stop "until their souls catch up with their bodies."[7] In our hectic, fast-paced lives, a daily devotional time allows our souls to catch up with our bodies. When that occurs, next-level influence is possible.

Being busy for kingdom purposes is no substitute for time spent with God. Billy Graham understands that perfectly. That is why he would call for T. W. to come so the two of them could study Scripture and pray. Our time with God affects the spiritual realm of our lives and does things for us that we could never accomplish without it.

T. W. remarked that if he had it to do all over again, he would spend more time in the Scriptures. We often hear that from the greats of the faith. Why? They understand the utmost importance of a disciplined devotional life. William Wilberforce said, "I must secure more time for private devotions. I have been living far too public for me. The shortening of private devotions starves the soul."[8]

The daily discipline of Bible reading and praying becomes the rudder that guides every other area of our lives. Discipline in the matter of a daily devotional time promotes discipline in all other areas of life. This is the secret of a long next-level influence.

Many leaders who fail morally, especially in ministry, can trace the beginning of their downslide to an abandonment of a passionate devotional life. George Sweeting said, "If we don't maintain a quiet time each day, it's not really because we are too busy; it's because we do not feel it is important enough. There's an old navy rule: when ships readjust their compass, they drop anchor in a quiet place."[9]

4. Listening Attentively

The next-level influencer is a good listener. This is a rare commodity in our culture. T. W. Wilson knew Billy Graham so well he could often speak for him. He knew what Billy would have wanted in many situations.

A good listener listens with his entire body. He is intently focused upon the one talking. He is not easily distracted by what is going on around him. As Dean Rusk said, "The organ in our body that requires the most energy is not the heart or the brain, it is the inner ear."[10] Being a good listener is a learned skill. Listening demonstrates your concern for someone, and if a person knows you care, you have the opportunity for influence. "According to *Psychology Today*, ninety percent of those who go for counseling don't really want answers, they just want someone to hear them out and listen. People of our society hunger for relationships that will provide concern and understanding."[11] T. W. related this story concerning Johnny Cash and Billy Graham and the influence we can have when we listen: "It was in Knoxville, Tennessee, and Johnny Cash was talking with Mr. Graham and asked him, 'Billy, do you think a Christian ought to smoke?' Billy said, 'Well, Johnny, what do you think about it?' He thought a moment without saying a word, and then Billy said, 'Johnny, you've answered your own question.' Johnny looked at Billy and he said, 'I've smoked my last cigarette.'"

5. Be Available

Next-level influencers make themselves available to be used by God in the lives of people. That will mean at times having our schedules interrupted and being inconvenienced for the sake of someone else. Perhaps it is true that the best ability is availability, always watching for and being ready for that moment when God says, "Go for it."

Opportunities for next-level influence often come at "inconvenient" times—when we are tired, in the middle of the night, when we are busy doing something else, or when our schedule is beyond full. We must be sensitive to the voice of God as he leads us to spend time with someone or to approach someone.

T. W. Wilson's availability to Billy Graham knew no bounds. He also made himself available to the entire Billy Graham team, their family members, and anyone who said to him, "Could you help me?"

The next-level influencer makes himself or herself always available to hear from God. Gigi Graham Tchividjian, daughter of Billy and Ruth Graham, learned a wonderful insight from her busy mom. "My mother had five children and often didn't have time for long devotions. But I remember her Bible always open in a convenient place—the kitchen counter, her bedside table, beside the sofa, or even on the ironing board. In this way, she could quickly glean a promise or memorize a verse as she continued her work."[12] That's letting God influence you so you can influence others.

8

BOB HOPE, ROMANS 8:28

Next-Level Influencers Use Humor

Dr. Lewis Drummond, the late close friend of T. W. Wilson and noted scholar and author, said of T. W., "He's a spiritual Bob Hope." Several of T. W.'s friends also commented that T. W. looked a lot like Bob Hope. T. W. used one occasion to take advantage of the celebrity of his famous look-alike. T. W. and Billy Graham were on their way to a crusade, traveling on a little DC-3 that made lots of stops. T. W. happened to be wearing a black-and-white checked suit and a black hat. A number of people at that time thought he resembled Bob Hope. T. W. recalled what happened when the plane stopped in El Paso: "This fellow came up to me and he said, 'Excuse me, what is your name?' And I said, 'You don't know me.' And he said, 'Well, what is your name?' Billy, knowing who he thought I was, said, 'Oh, go ahead and tell him, Bob.' And I tell you, it was awful. I

115

wound up signing these autographs, 'Bob Hope.' Now, this is the odd thing—I signed, 'Bob Hope, Romans 8:28'!"

Billy Graham and Bob Hope were friends, and both had a passion for golf. T. W. remembered walking along with Billy and Bob on the golf course. Both men had hit bad drives, and their balls were over in the edge of the woods. Bob hollered out to Billy, "Hey, Billy, help! I'm in trouble!"

T. W. tells what happened next: "I'm not exaggerating a bit. Billy, whose ball was over in the edge of the woods, hit the ball, and it wasn't a good hit. And it hit the water, and bounced off, and went right on the green about four to five feet from the hole, and of course Billy won the hole.

"That night Bob Hope said to an audience, 'I played golf with Billy Graham today and he really taught me a lesson. His golf ball walked on water.'"

T. W. shared his "grasshopper" experience in Northeast India during a crusade. They were guests in the home of the leader of that particular region. T. W. told the story: "Cliff Barrows was there, and he preached right after Billy, and then they wanted me to preach too. They kept bringing these things around here for us to eat them. I was going to grab them, and I would put them in the pocket of my coat, knowing that when I got home I could get my suit cleaned. I wasn't going to eat them. But then whatever his title was, the big shot, Cliff, and I sat down. I looked and there he was, and he said, 'I want to see how you like these.' I didn't know what to do, and I thought, *Whatever he feeds me, I will swallow.* I'll tell you the truth—now, you think I'm exaggerating, but it tasted pretty good."

On another occasion earlier in their ministry, Cliff, Billy, and T. W. were at a Youth for Christ meeting in Chicago. They all roomed together. T. W. and Cliff got to the room first and short-sheeted Billy. They also took the rollers off his bed, which was a roll-away bed. When Billy came in late, he sat on the bed and it fell. Cliff started laughing. Billy put Cliff in the bed and folded it up. When he did that, it hit the mirror and then Billy wanted to hit Cliff.

The Famous Georgia Pit Stop Experience

Cliff Barrows shared his version of an oft-told incident that happened to Billy and T. W. as they were traveling back to Montreat. This story made T famous—or infamous, depending on who you ask! Cliff said, "Billy from time to time has had threats on his life, which they have had to take seriously. Billy was in Hawaii; T. W. was with him; and Billy was not feeling well but finally getting strong enough to come home. A police chief, Dan Lieu . . . was on the Honolulu radio board of which T. W. was the chairman. So he was very close to them while they were over there, providing any kind of security they thought they needed. He put [Billy] on the plane to fly to Los Angeles. Just before they left Honolulu, or after they got to Los Angeles, they got word of another threat on his life.

"The police have to take it seriously, so they had arrangements for people to meet the plane and transport Billy to the next flight or whatever it was. Billy had asked T to call home to tell Ruth that they were on the way, and then Ruth said, 'Well, T, we have a new unlisted number, so write it down.'

"So I guess T wrote it down and gave it to Billy, and Billy just shoved it in his pocket. They got to Atlanta. It was a cold, wet, rainy night, and the flights were canceled into Greenville or wherever they were to land, and so Billy decided, 'T, let's drive a car. You drive, and I'll crawl in the backseat and sleep until we get home.' T said, 'Fine.' So he made arrangements. I think they rented a Cadillac; they never did rent them back then, but he wanted a heavy car so he could stretch out.

"So Billy took a sleeping pill and crawled in the back and had his coat and hat back there. T. W. took off. He was a good driver; he was a fast driver. Back in those days they didn't have I-85; they had four lanes, but it was not like it is now. They had a highway that the locals call 'the Woodpecker Trail,' which cut off and went through the country and went into Greenville, but it was not like it is today, obviously.

"T thought he knew where the turnoff was, so he took it. When they got down the road, he still wasn't quite so sure. They came to Jefferson, Georgia, where there was a little roadside stand, a little restaurant, and it had a little restroom along the side, and the light was on. T called back and said, 'Buddy, I'm going to stop here for a minute and make sure the directions are right.' He didn't hear any noises, so he looked back and assumed Billy was asleep. He pulled in, windshield wipers going, and left the car running. T ran through the rain, to the restaurant, to get directions.

"While he was out that split second, Billy thought he needed to use the facility, so he jumped out of the car without his coat and ran to the little restroom. While he was in the restroom, T came out of the restaurant, ran through the rain, jumped in the car, said, 'Buddy, we're on the right track, and we'll be in Greenville in an hour and a half,' and he took off. The coat was back there with the hat, and he didn't bother to check, but he thought [Billy] was in there.

"Well, Billy comes out of the washhouse and looks and T's heading down the road, and all he sees are the red lights disappearing. Billy's name was well known, so he went into the restaurant.

It was just an old country restaurant; a couple of old truck drivers were there. He didn't have much money, he didn't have his coat, and he was cold. Finally he said, 'Is there anybody here that can help me catch that guy? He ran off without me.'

"There was nobody there who would even try to catch him, nobody who could catch him anyway. So he thought, 'Well, surely he'll turn around and see that I'm not there, and he'll come back.' Billy identified himself, and they said, 'Yeah, sure.' They didn't believe that he was Billy Graham. He was there without a coat, and his buddy had left him.

"While he was in this little restaurant, Billy tried to call home, but the new number was in his coat pocket, and he didn't have his coat. He said to the operator, 'Operator, I'm Billy Graham. I need to call home. My wife doesn't know where I am and I need to talk to her.' She said, 'Well, sir, I don't doubt you if you tell me you're Billy Graham, but I cannot give you the number.' They wouldn't give him the number.

"Billy, while waiting, ordered a bowl of bean soup and sat there and ate it. Finally he said, 'Is there anybody here who will drive me to Greenville?' Well, that was quite a drive, I'll tell you, and the weather was bad.

"Finally one old boy said, 'Yeah, I'll take you to Greenville.' It was a pickup, and the windshield was cracked on it. He was a country soul. They got in the truck, and Billy kept watching every car that passed. This driver thought he was 'on the run' from the law. Billy was hoping T. W. had alerted the highway patrol and they'd be coming back trying to find him.

"When T. W. got to Greenville, he just said, 'Buddy, we're in Greenville. Do you want to stop and get something to eat?' There was no sound. He thought, 'Bless his heart, he's really out.' So he went right on through, and he got to Asheville, then to Montreat, and he said, 'Well, I've got to stop and get some gas.'

"When T. W. got out of the car in Black Mountain to get gas, he looked back there and there was no Billy. He thought, 'What in the world? Where did he go?' Well, there was a threat on his life, and the rapture, but he thought, 'Well, I'm as ready to go in the rapture as he is,' so he kind of dismissed that, but it really bugged him.

"This is the way I remember it. T. W. called Ruth, and he said, 'Ruth, have you seen Billy? Have you heard from Billy?' She said, 'What do you mean, "Have I seen Billy?" He's with you!' T. W. said, 'Well, he was, but he isn't now.' They had also called Ruth about the threat on his life, and the children had heard. And now here T. W. was showing up, Billy not feeling well, hadn't seen him for the last two and a half or three hours from Atlanta, and he gets there and he's gone.

"Well, they tried to retrace every exit, called the local police. T. W. was in good standing with all the local cops. They got on their car radios, and they radioed back and forth to the Georgia State Police. Of course, they didn't know he'd gotten in a truck and gotten to Greenville.

"Billy got to the Holiday Inn in Greenville and paid the man, but the man still didn't believe it was Billy Graham, and he made him get out.

"He brought the manager of the Holiday Inn out to the car, to identify him. 'Yeah, I know him well.' But he didn't have a single room in that hotel. He said, 'Billy, I'll give you my office; we'll put a bed up here.' Billy was so disgusted and tired, he said, 'No, just drive me to the airport if you will, Bob.' His name was Bob Green. 'Let me rent a car and I'll drive home.'

"Well, the drive from Greenville to Asheville in those days was one of the worst drives in the country, with those winding roads. Well, Billy finally, dead tired, at two or three in the morning, pulled in up at the house. Of course, there was great relief, and Billy said, 'Thank ya, pal.'

"T often reminded Billy Graham that he didn't leave him, Billy left T. W.! Well, T's never lived that down. At the Baptist World Alliance in Miami, Florida, Mr. Graham met the Russian delegation, who asked what became of the man who left him in Georgia. Billy said, 'He's right over there.' They said, 'You mean he's still with you? In Russia that would not be the case!'"

Matching Practical Jokes with Ruth Graham

During a time when UFO sightings were being reported throughout the country, Ruth and T. W. traded practical jokes.

It began with T. W. calling Ruth excitedly, telling her to rush out and see the UFO in the sky near the mountain ridge. Ruth called Ned, the youngest of the Graham children, who was the only one at home, and they hurried outside but could find nothing.

Unwilling to be bested by T. W., Ruth told Ned to scream like a banshee while she called T. W. Ruth shouted into the telephone, "It's landing in our yard!" and slammed down the receiver. Then she and Ned went out to sit on the steps and listen to T. W.'s car tires squealing as his car hurled up the mountain, careening around the mountain curves, and braked to a sudden stop in the driveway. It was April 1, so she said, "April Fools!"

T. W. was incensed. He told Ruth that not only had he and Glenn Wilcox, who was with him at the time, seen the UFO, but that several neighbors had also witnessed it. Finally even Ruth was convinced they'd seen some strange object, but T. W. was still a little miffed. As he started home he said to Ruth from the car window, "Even if one should land in your yard, don't call me."[1]

T. W. was not to be outdone by Ruth. Mary Helen Wilson shares another story: "Someone called from the Graham home and said somebody was having a baby. T was told, 'Get a doctor up here right now.' Well, T smelled a rat. He knew it was going to be a joke, and Glen Matter and his wife were eating lunch with us. And he said, 'Come on, Glen.' He was a little short, very distinguished man—he looked like a doctor. And he went. They walked in the door and T said, 'Here's the doctor—where's the patient?'"

T. W. picked up the story and gave the specifics: "Zinny called and said, 'Dr. Wilson?' And I said, 'Yes.' And she said, 'Can you come up here? There's a baby fixin' to be born,' . . . and I recognized the voice. . . . I said, 'Well, thank you very much; I'll get there as quickly as I can.'

"I said to our lunch guest, 'Glen, I want you to help me play a trick.' He had white hair and he looked like a medical doctor. Well, his wife had a bag about like Mary Helen has, a big purse, and I said, 'I want you to get that, and we're going to rush up there.' I went on up there and I said, 'Anne, where's the patient?' She didn't know what to say. I said, 'Well, I have the doctor here. They called here and said that there is a baby getting ready to be born and they wanted me to get the doctor,' and I said, 'I have Dr. Matter.' Anne said, 'Uh . . .' Then I saw Zinny. I said, 'Well, where's the patient?'

"So I went into the dining room area, which is in the middle of their house, and Ruth was in there with two ladies, and of course I knew that it was all a joke. So I said, 'Pardon me, Ruth; I'm sorry, but I have the doctor here, and I wanted to know, where's the patient?' She looked at me. She's always playing tricks, you know. She said, 'T, are you serious?' I said, 'Well, they called from here. Zinny called and said that they wanted me to bring the doctor, there's a baby getting ready to be born, and I have Dr. Matter with me.'

"She said, 'T, can't you take a joke?' I said, 'A joke?' I looked at Glen and I said, 'Well, Doctor, I'm embarrassed, and I apologize, but that's all right. We'll take care of you, Doctor.' Ruth didn't know what to say. I could write a book on tricks Ruth has played on people, and I enjoyed getting one on her!"

The Fuller Brush Days and Other Light Moments

T. W. and Grady Wilson and Billy Graham were all Fuller Brush salesmen. In a letter on Youth for Christ stationery, Billy Graham mentions a "bed bug" experience that occurred during one of their assignments as salesmen. T. W. explained, "It was just Billy, Grady, and me, and we were staying in a hotel room with no air-conditioning. It was in Monroe, North Carolina, and we couldn't afford a room with two beds, so Billy and I had to sleep in a double bed. It was as cheap as we could get by. It was way before daylight and Billy hollered out, 'Turn on the light!' Then I heard *slap!*, followed by 'I got it.' We all thought it was a mosquito. So when we turned on the light, we had been hitting not mosquitoes but bed bugs. An evangelist friend, Jimmie Johnson, was having a meeting in Monroe, and a big tent had been set up with a sawdust floor. We left the hotel and made our beds on sawdust."

T. W. related this comical moment about a trip to England: "I think it was Sheffield. We stayed in a Holiday Inn which was right next to a pasture—a cow pasture—and of course Billy, being reared on a farm, . . . would go out there every day. . . . We'd go for a walk, and then he'd go [over to the] cattle out there, and he'd say, 'Moo-o-o-o, moo-o-o-o, moo-o-o-o,' and man, they'd come running. I mean, they'd come over to the fence, every day; it was just standard procedure.

"The Duke and Duchess lived right near where we stayed, but that didn't stop Billy from calling the cows. So Billy, from his room, would call the cattle . . . and boy, they'd come running at night . . .

"This only goes to prove: you can take the boys out of North Carolina, but you can't take North Carolina out of the boys."

George Beverly Shea related the following: "It was the Winnipeg crusade, many years ago. Billy was speaking on the Holy Spirit. Mr. Graham has certain songs that he expects me to sing, twelve or fifteen. If I get out of that, he may not say anything, but I know he wants me to stay in that, so I chose one that night. The words were, 'Holy Spirit, please provide, ever near the Christian side . . .'

"I got to the parking lot and T. W. says, 'Hey, Bev. . . . That was great tonight, but you know Billy likes the old songs.' I said, 'Well, T. W., that was written at the turn of the century.' He laughed and he said, 'That's okay.'"

The Power of Humor

Next-level influencers know how to include humor to move people in a God-ward direction. This is not a silly giddiness that laughs at every issue but using humor at appropriate times in order to persuade people toward our faith. So often Christianity has been characterized as humorless, and many of those who follow the name of Christ have not helped to change that characterization. This is certainly not what the Bible teaches. "A joyful heart is good medicine" (Prov. 17:22). Christianity is the faith of the joyful heart. Next-level influencers intend to infect the world with that joy. Consider these lessons on next-level influence.

1. Make Humor Your Friend

Next-level influencers see the lighter side of life. They don't find it a scriptural contradiction to laugh. Learning to laugh at yourself is one of the best gifts you can give yourself.

People tend to be more comfortable around those with a sense of humor. They tend to be more willing to open up and let their guard down.

In 1981, when President Ronald Reagan was shot by John Hinckley and rushed to the hospital in serious condition, he said to the doctors, "I hope you're Republicans!" By using humor he brought a sense of hope to a difficult situation. We tend to remember those people we have met who possess a good sense of humor. When we are remembered, our message is not forgotten.

Being a next-level influencer is not about winning a popularity contest. It does, however, matter that people like us, and those with a good sense of humor are more likeable. When you can laugh at yourself and with people, it makes you more human, touchable, and accessible. People are more likely to lend you their ears. Charles M. Schulz, creator of *Peanuts*, noted, "No one would have been invited to dinner as often as Jesus was unless he was interesting and had a good sense of humor."[2] Next-level influencers have given themselves permission to enjoy life.

2. Humor Dispels the Myths about Our Faith

The next-level influencer uses humor to dispel some myths concerning Christianity. Unfortunately, the caricature of the Christian has been a solemn, rules-driven, never-have-any-fun, unhappy person with an aversion to laughing. No wonder the world is turned off to Christ—people are turned off to what they see in too many Christians.

The next-level influencer is committed to changing that caricature. When a Christian possesses a good sense of humor, that can become attractive to those who do not know Christ.

People are drawn to those who can see the lighter side of life. This works in any language since laughter has no accent. Humor is mobile; it can go with you anywhere. It will work in any situation or any location. When people saw that the team members of the Billy Graham Evangelistic Association could laugh at themselves and have fun along the way, it spoke volumes as to the legitimacy of their faith and message.

3. Humor Makes a Point

Next-level influencers often use humor to get their point across. People are more apt to listen to what we have to say when the right amount of humor is injected into the conversation or presentation. Herbert Gardner said, "Once you get people laughing, they're listening and you can tell them almost anything."[3] As Victor Borge said, "Laughter is the shortest distance between two people."[4]

Someone once said, "A good sense of humor helps to overlook the unbecoming, understand the unconventional, tolerate the unpleasant, overcome the unexpected, and outlast the unbearable."[5] Another advantage to using the right amount of humor is that it can defuse a tense situation.

Sometimes just a one-liner, like T. W. used on many occasions, can make all the difference. Humor can be a pause button to allow everyone to regain the right perspective. However, this doesn't mean you should be a walking fountain of one-liners. Sometimes humor is not appropriate, and too much humor can be worse than no humor at all.

4. Humor Brings Relief from Stress

The next-level influencer uses humor to relieve stress. Those who are committed to changing the world are often faced with stress due to the demands upon their time and emotions. Next-level influencers often become drained both physically and emotionally. President Dwight D. Eisenhower said, "Laughter can relieve tension, soothe the pain of disappointment, and strengthen the spirit for the formidable tasks that always lie ahead."[6] Abraham Lincoln, during the difficult days of the Civil War, said, "With the fearful strain that is on me day and night, if I did not laugh, I should die."[7]

According to a study conducted by the University of Maryland in Baltimore, "Laughter releases chemicals into the bloodstream that relax the blood vessels. In addition, hearty laughter reduces blood pressure and heart rate."[8] Dr. Michael Miller, who is the director of the Center for Preventive Cardiology at the university, interviewed 150 patients who had suffered heart troubles and 150 who had not. Patients were asked questions to measure their response in typical day-to-day situations. The results showed that individuals with heart problems were 40 per cent less likely to respond with laughter.[9]

Next-level influencers are in the heart business—the business of changing the heart spiritually. Laughter becomes one of our greatest allies in helping to present a message that will heal the heart.

9

SHHH! DON'T TELL

*Next-Level Influencers
Keep Confidences*

The Duke of Wellington is best remembered as the general who defeated Napoleon at Waterloo in 1815. During his earlier service in India, Wellington was in charge of negotiations after the battle of Assaye. The emissary of an Indian ruler, anxious to know what territories would be ceded to his master, tried in various ways to get the information. Finally, he offered Wellington a large sum of money. 'Can you keep a secret?' asked Wellington. 'Yes indeed,' the man said eagerly. 'So can I,' he replied."[1]

Keeping a confidence is the cement that holds souls together. Relationships have been destroyed because someone failed to keep his lips zipped. When that happens, not only is the person who shared confidential information hurt, but the credibility of the one who shared is also destroyed. Many times other people are hurt too. In some cases, it could do irreparable damage to the cause of Christ. Unfortunately, sharing a confidence has often been masked in spiritual language such as a prayer request or expressing a concern over someone.

Billy Graham chose well the one in whom he would share confidences. He knew that he could share absolutely anything with T and never worry about it being repeated. It is a godly discipline to be able to resist telling when someone says, "Don't tell." In the hours I spent in interviewing T. W., I could tell there were some things he would take to the grave with him, and he did. Not that those things were negative—he was simply honoring his word that some things need to be kept between friends.

T. W. was never negative about Mr. Graham or anyone on the Billy Graham Evangelistic Association team. He showed the utmost respect for each member of the team. T heard a lot of things from people all over the world in his almost forty years with Billy Graham. Those things he heard that needed to be shared with Billy were shared, but many of those things were not, because T. W. didn't traffic in gossip and rumors—only truth, and only that which was necessary to protect Mr. Graham's laser-beam focus on sharing the gospel.

In that respect, Billy Graham could not have had a better confidant. The evangelist knew he needed someone with whom he could bare his soul and, when needed, vent his frustrations. Billy Graham is the first to admit, "I am human." T. W. allowed him to be human, and that was always safe. T. W. knew as much as anyone about Billy Graham—his thoughts, his attitudes, his feelings, his struggles, his anxieties—yet he never felt he had to one-up his friend. He never gave the sense of *I-know-something-you-don't-know*, nor did he ever have the feeling that Billy owed him something. T. W. didn't lose the sense of loyalty and utmost respect for his friend.

Evangelist Luis Palau offered his insight about how T. W. could keep a confidence: "I'm sure he heard, saw, all sorts of stuff, but he just let it go, like one should. He always blessed you, always encouraged you; he never got negative, he never gossiped. I never heard him, in all the years I hung around."

T. W. knew many things that would compromise Billy Graham's safety and security if shared. For instance, during a crusade Billy Graham is, by necessity, booked in a hotel or place not made known to the public. Obviously if his location were made known, he would not be able to rest prior to the crusade. The media would have come looking for him. So who knew where Billy Graham was staying? T. W. Wilson knew because he had personally made the arrangements.

Fooling the Press in NYC

Billy and T. W. were in New York City for a meeting when T. W. discovered that President Richard Nixon was in the hospital with a serious condition. T. W. told Billy, and Billy said, "We need to go see him." Wilson went to work.

Billy made a few calls, and T. W. arranged for a taxi to take them to the hospital. There a waiting crowd recognized Billy. T. W. hustled him into the hospital. Billy was unable to see the president because of his condition, but he did visit with Tricia (Mr. Nixon's daughter) and her husband.

After Billy talked and prayed with the family, T. W. spoke with the hospital administrator and asked, "Is there any way I can get Dr. Graham out of here without going through those press people out there?" He said, "Yes." T. W. said, "Would you be kind enough to go out there and tell that taxi driver where to go? Don't let anybody hear you; just tell him where to go." The paper the next morning said, "Billy Graham spent the night at the hospital."

Keeping a Confidence from Billy Graham

Some things T. W. knew were better left unknown by Billy Graham. That took discernment on T's part. Those confidences helped protect Billy from unnecessary worry and distractions. Billy was unaware of most of the security threats.

At times Billy Graham didn't feel well or was exhausted both physically and emotionally, pulled in a dozen different directions, with the burden of the world on his heart. T. W. was always there to encourage him and to make sure that Mr. Graham's physical needs received attention. He jealously guarded his health.

T. W. had to make discerning calls often as the gatekeeper of who was able to see Mr. Graham. Cliff Barrows noted how well T. W. could get to the heart of a matter to decide what needed Billy's attention: "Well, obviously he's been a good representative, because of his friendliness, his burden for souls, his passion to preach, and the message of the evangelist. He was more than qualified in all of those areas. But he has been a good gatekeeper and a good person to help, protect, and to build an entree for the people that Billy wants and needs to see. It took someone who knew a lot about the background of the people. Either men in politics, or preachers particularly, T would know the background of the people and he would give Billy the information.

He could get information for Billy that nobody else could get, by just the sensitivity and the feelers he had out and the way he could read people."

After Billy accepted the presidency of Northwestern Schools in Minneapolis, Minnesota, he immediately turned to T. W. for help. But T. W. kept him waiting for an answer. He said, "It was before I was thirty. Billy stayed on my neck for I don't know how long, wanting me to go with him to Northwestern.

"I said, 'Look, I know my weaknesses, and I am not a college vice president.' He said, 'Yeah, but we could build a great school there.' I said, 'We?' So every night for about ten nights, wherever he was, he called me. I answered the phone, 'Billy,' because I always thought it was him on the phone. Whenever he called he would always say, 'Have you prayed about it?' He finally persuaded me to consider the opportunity. Mary Helen was willing if I believed I was in God's will. We had several wonderful but difficult years in Minneapolis."

The administrative experience that T. W. gained would prove to be invaluable in the years to come.

The Power of Keeping Confidences

Next-level influence depends on one's ability to keep a confidence. T. W. Wilson said, "When people trust you enough to give you a confidential piece of information, if you cannot be trusted to keep that, you lose your integrity and you lose your ability to be trusted. And it doesn't take long for people to find out the truth." *The Message* paraphrase puts it this way: "Gossips can't keep secrets, so never confide in blabbermouths" (Prov. 20:19).

We tend to be influenced by those whom we can trust. With that trust comes many opportunities to impact people for God. Furthermore, when we choose to be confidence-keeping people, we gain a lot of knowledge—knowledge we can use to become more effective in life. Those who can trust us with confidences normally grant us permission to advise them. Those private times create an atmosphere where next-level influence can happen. Consider the following lessons of next-level influence.

1. A Confidence Keeper

Next-level influence includes the ability to keep a confidence; nothing will influence a person more than knowing you kept his confidence. It is a sacred trust between two people. When someone says, "Don't tell," you don't tell. Keeping a confidence is a choice and a discipline. In other words, it is learned. James knew we would have a struggle in this area, and that is why he told us that outside of Christ's control, the tongue is extremely dangerous. "For we all stumble in many ways. If anyone does not stumble in what he says, he is a perfect man, able to bridle the whole body as well" (James 3:2).

Billy Graham's safety and ministry effectiveness depended upon T. W. Wilson's decision to keep confidences. You may not be protecting Billy Graham, but anyone's reputation is worthy of keeping a confidence. Each of us needs someone with whom we can unload and explode.

The importance of one keeping a confidence cannot be overstated. "Don't tell anyone" means just that. People who can keep our confidences also influence us. "He who goes about as a talebearer reveals secrets, but he who is trustworthy conceals a matter" (Prov. 11:13). We must never be like Dennis of *Dennis the Menace*. In one comic strip Dennis is whispering in the ear of the man next door, "Now listen good. I can only tell this once 'cause my dad told me not to repeat it."[2]

The next-level influencer understands that personal and private things shared with him do not belong to him to share with anyone else. If the person who is sharing the confidence wishes to share that confidence with others, that is his prerogative; however, the next-level influencer possesses no such right. We all know things which if shared could be hurtful to the innocent, negative without intending to be, misunderstood by the unknowing, injurious to those who need to be protected, damaging to a cause, or compromising of safety and security.

2. Refuses to Sacrifice a Confidence for Fame or Gain

Next-level influencers are out to impact people, not to seek personal gain. They keep a confidence because it is the right thing to do. They are out to help people, not to gain notoriety. Keeping a confidence is a great form of humility. Often those who share what they shouldn't do so in an attempt to impress others. Those who keep a confidence experience great joy and satisfaction but never boast about what they know. They stand in contrast to those who have had close personal relationships with famous people and have betrayed a confidence by giving in to the temptation to give a tell-all interview or write a book for notoriety or financial gain.

Reputations have been tarnished and lives destroyed because someone close to a well-known person wanted a few minutes of fame. Next-level influencers cannot be bought for any price.

3. *The Privilege of Intercession*

Because they are privy to information about a person, next-level influencers can become much more effective intercessors. They know better how to pray for the person. Prayer is the greatest influencer in the world. When we possess a confidence from someone, we are in a privileged position—but more importantly, a responsible position. John Calvin said, "To make intercession for men is the most powerful and practical way in which we can express our love for them."[3] Knowing a confidence should always drive us to our knees for that person. Even after retiring from traveling with Billy Graham, T. W. continued interceding for his friend until he died. He took Billy's confidences to the grave with him, but he thoroughly bombarded heaven on behalf of Billy and his ministry while alive.

Intercessory prayer is often preceded by a burden to pray for that person. You can't get that person out of your mind, or you have a "divine impression" to immediately start interceding in prayer.

There have been numerous times in my life when I was facing unknown dangers, unannounced testing times, or traps set by Satan to distract me or detour me from the path of God's will. Then out of nowhere an email comes, the phone rings, or a letter arrives, and God, at the exact moment I needed it, burdened someone to pray for me. There are times I am not sure why, nor does the person God prompted to pray for me know why at the moment, but prayer prevented something from happening that could have hurt me or the cause of Christ. There are times when I discovered later that the exact instant when a person prayed for me was the moment I was facing an impeding danger. One day in heaven we will joyfully discover how the intercession of specific people whom God burdened placed a hedge of protection around us. One of the greatest blessings we can give to another is taking time to pray on their behalf. No wonder Samuel said, "Moreover, as for me, far be it from me that I should sin against the Lord by ceasing to pray for you" (1 Sam. 12:23).

Our intercession on behalf of others may save their lives, or it may protect or deliver them from the fiery furnace of temptation, danger, or undetected traps set by the enemy.

4. Protects People from Unnecessary Worry

Next-level influencers don't feel the need to share everything they know. If something can be left unsaid that will prevent someone from experiencing undue worry, they don't say it. T. W. Wilson kept many things from Mr. Graham so as not to worry him or distract him from his central purpose of preaching the gospel. If something needed to be shared with Billy, he didn't hesitate, but if it was not necessary, T kept it to himself. The next-level influencer is sensitive to sharing anything that could potentially hurt someone.

Proverbs says, "Death and life are in the power of the tongue" (Prov. 18:21). As much as the tongue can bring life, it can also bring death to joy or to someone's reputation. Consider making every word pass through the THINK gate. Is it *True*? Is it *Helpful*? Is it *Integrity* driven? Is it *Necessary*? Is it *Kind*? If your words can't pass this test, those words are better left unsaid.

This is why T. W. Wilson could be the gatekeeper to Billy Graham. He didn't want to shelter him, for Billy loves being with people, but he did want to protect him from that which was not essential.

5. *Not an Occasion for Lectures*

The next-level encourager won't use a confidence someone shares as an occasion to lecture the person or give an "I told you so" speech. Offering a piece of advice or giving an opinion is far different than making the person feel he or she is getting a lecture. In all honesty, we simply don't know what we would do if we were in that person's set of circumstances. A confidence is never used against that person in any way.

When someone shares a confidence, the next-level influencer has to determine, *Is this person sharing something that he simply wants to get off his chest, or is this person in trouble? Is he sharing something that indicates a problem that I need to do something about and should suggest an action for, or is it simply an issue he doesn't want the burden of bearing alone?* It will require the wisdom of God to know the difference.

6. *Despises Gossip*

You simply can't be a next-level influencer and be a gossip too. Being a gossip cancels out any influence one might have. Most of us have experienced gossip being shared about us. When that happens, darts of betrayal, anger, disappointment, and sorrow penetrate our minds and hearts. T. W. Wilson never gossiped about anyone. Even when he shared stories for this book, he made it clear that he was in no way sharing a confidence. At times he would begin a story and then say, "No, I'm not going to share that." Even after his debilitating stroke, he never let something slip that was supposed to be kept confidential.

The entire Billy Graham Evangelistic Association team has the same kind of ability to keep confidences and never resort to gossip. When a problem arose, rather than discussing it with other people, T. W. dealt with it head-on with the individual and then didn't bring it up again. When rumors circulated, he immediately got to the source and the truth of it.

Dr. John Skowronski, a psychology professor at Ohio State University, was the lead author of a study that assessed the effects of gossip. They discovered that people who hear your gossip will actually associate the message with you. If you talk about someone who is dishonest, the person hearing you tell the story will associate that characteristic with you as well. Likewise, if you sing the praises of someone who is getting a degree from Harvard, you will be remembered as intellectual.

Dr. Skowronski said, "It's a memory mistake. You listen to the descriptions of others' actions without thinking much about it. Later, when you search your thoughts about the person who told you, you subconsciously associate them with their description of someone else."[4] The Bible revealed that fact years before. "Let no unwholesome word proceed from your mouth, but only such a word as is good for edification according to the need of the moment, so that it will give grace to those who hear" (Eph. 4:29).

10

The Accountability Factor

*Next-Level Influencers
Have Accountability*

Accountability can make a ministry or break a ministry. With it, one's testimony can remain sterling; without it, a reputation can be destroyed.

Accountability means we choose to put ourselves under the authority of someone or certain people. Accountability means granting permission to that person or those people to ask us the hard questions. Furthermore, it provides an opportunity for us to give an answer for what we say or do. T. W. Wilson was not uncomfortable asking people the hard questions, whether it was to determine why someone needed to see or talk to Billy Graham, discern if a need was legitimate and immediate, or decide if he needed to ask his friend Billy Graham a difficult question. If he thought that Billy needed to think further about a situation, he would ask him to make sure he had thought it through.

Billy Graham and T. W. Wilson had freedom within their relationship to discuss anything. It was T's goal to make Billy the very best he could be, with no personal ambitions ever getting in the way. This high accountability has kept the Billy Graham Evangelistic Association's impeccable reputation intact through all these years.

T. W. Wilson's standards of morality reached the highest level, and he made sure that wherever he went, he had people around him who held the same standards. When people represent God, they must incorporate into their lives standards that the world may think are extreme yet are necessary in order to protect their reputation and, more importantly, Christ's reputation.

T. W. and Billy's late physician, Dr. Roger James, said, "They are brothers in Christ, of course, but they're almost like brothers, they are so close. They've been together for so long, the right hand knows what the left hand is going to do. It's like when you play tennis; you want to know where your partner is. Well, they're going to know where each other is, what they're thinking, and what they're going to do next. T. W. can anticipate Billy like nobody can anticipate what he's going to do, because he's seen him for fifty years, and he's been in action with him."

Billy Graham needed T. W., and he was the first to admit it. It is a sign of strength, not weakness, when we can admit we need someone to pray for us, hold us accountable, and share the journey. We need someone with whom we can laugh and cry. Often, accountability begins with a relationship. The following story illustrates one of the many relationship memories T. W. had with Billy.

The accountability began between T. W. and Billy during their college days. T. W. shared a story about Billy's father giving him, Billy, and Grady a job loading a truck. T. W. remembers: "Grady and Billy had the hard job; they had to stick it up there when I had to get it up on the truck. It was falling all down on me. Well, anyway, it was hot, real hot, and Billy was about to faint. He said, 'I can't stand this heat; it's got me.' And Grady said, 'Well, I feel kind of bad myself,' so I went inside and I told Mr. Graham, 'Mr. Graham, have you not got two big husky boys that you could put up there to do that job?'

"And so later on Grady said, 'Billy, do you remember anything like that?' And Billy said, 'No, I don't remember anything like that.' And they said, 'You know, T can really make up a lot of stuff like that.'"

T. W. and Billy teased about this incident for years.

Scandal Proof

Why has the Billy Graham Evangelistic Association team for years lived above moral scandal and accusations of improprieties? Obviously many reasons could be listed, but the number one reason can be summed up in the word *accountability*. The organization has simply no tolerance for compromise spiritually, morally, or ethically.

The strength of a real accountability relationship is that it weathers the storms of time. It is stronger than the trials that come and more resilient than a wrong attitude. Simply put, it hangs in there no matter what. Jim Wilson said of his father's long friendship with Billy Graham, "One of the first things that I think of with my dad is that he is a man of great principle . . . and that involves integrity. . . . People will say, 'How has Billy Graham survived all these years without any taint of scandal when it seems like a lot of these television preachers and big names seem to fall?'

"Well, Billy was a man of integrity, and he put himself under accountability. Not the least of that process of accountability was who he surrounded himself with . . . and my dad has been one of the key figures in there. I've heard my dad say, kind of humorously, 'For Billy to sin, at least some moral sin, it would take a conspiracy.' He said, 'He can't do anything without me.' That was back when he traveled every minute with Billy. He said, 'For him to do anything, I'd have to agree to it. And he knows that's not going to happen.'

"So there has been a tremendous accountability and integrity with the inner circle of this group. And that's the reason God has given such longevity. I think Daddy has become more diplomatic as the years have gone by. He's been more compassionate; he was more passionate . . . and now that passion is combined with compassion. . . . He has a great deal of compassion. I've seen him just weep over things . . . but I really believe that Daddy, even at this stage, he would stand—if he felt like he was the only one standing on an issue, he would stand. He doesn't mind being the only one, if he has to. It's just amazing, that integrity, that strength."

Billy Sunday's Music Director

Accountability ran deep within T. W. He not only kept himself accountable but helped those he was close to be accountable too. He didn't do this because he felt he was the spiritual police for everyone; he just loved his friends so much that he didn't want to see anything happen to their credibility.

Sometimes T. W. and Homer Rodeheaver would conduct evangelistic meetings together. They were very close friends. Mr. Rodeheaver was the music director for the famous evangelist Billy Sunday. He was legendary.

At one meeting a young lady apparently had her eyes on Rodeheaver. T. W. remembered: "He came by my room and he said, 'I'm being tempted by this lady.' I said, 'Rodie, what do you think she's interested in? Could it be your name, your money, or your food?' See, he was eighty-something; he could hardly carry a tune then, but his name recognition was still strong. 'Why should she come quite a distance to see you?' I said. 'Let me ask you a question: are you wanting me to agree with you, or are you wanting me to tell you, honestly, what I think?' He said, 'No, I want you to tell me honestly what you think.' I said to him, 'I think you already know.' He said, 'T. W., you are a very wise man.'"

In an interview in his home, Billy Graham expressed his "utmost love, admiration, and gratefulness" to the man who had been his accountability partner all these years. T. W. felt that "retirement" should not be in a Christian's vocabulary. He dreaded it. God took him home to heaven one week to the day from when he was supposed to retire.

The Power of Accountability

Personal accountability determines the strength of public accountability. When we are committed to doing what is right when the public can't see us, the likelihood that we will do what is right when the public *can* see us increases dramatically. However, when one is only publicly accountable and not privately accountable, that will soon be revealed. It happens in businesses, marriages, and ministries. The strength of the Billy Graham team has its foundation in a tight accountability to each other. They have made a commitment to hold each other accountable and not to criticize people publicly or become defensive because of criticism.

T. W. gave his version of an occasion where this commitment was put into practice: "At a press conference, this one fellow stood up and he was a pressman, he didn't believe anything. . . . He said, 'Billy Graham, there was a well-known preacher that told me something yesterday, and I'd like to hear your comment. He said, "You set the church back a hundred or maybe two hundred years." What have you got to say about that?' And Billy bowed his head a minute. He said, 'I feel like apologizing to the Lord, because when I came here, I prayed that the Lord would set the church back two thousand years.' That fellow, you couldn't see him. He sank deeper and deeper. And let me tell you what the response was—this was the secular press, and when he said that, they began to applaud."

Scientists now say that a series of slits, not a giant gash, sank the *Titanic*. The opulent, nine-hundred-foot cruise ship sank in 1912 on its first voyage, traveling from England to New York. The worst maritime disaster of the time took the lives of fifteen hundred people. The most widely held theory is that the ship hit an iceberg, which opened a huge gash in the side of the liner.

In August of 1996, an international team of divers and scientists used sound waves to probe through the wreckage, buried in mud two and one-half miles down in the North Atlantic. Their discovery? The damage was surprisingly small. Instead of the huge gash, they found six relatively narrow slits across the six watertight holds. "Everything that could go wrong did," said William Garzke Jr., a naval architect who helped the team with their analysis.[1]

Something little, over time, can destroy not only a ship but a life. Solomon spoke of "the little foxes that are ruining the vineyards" (Song of Sol. 2:15). We must guard ourselves against those little things, such as little compromises and moral short-cuts, that could damage our walk with God.

Next-level influence depends upon accountability. We have seen the results of failure to be accountable. Whether it is Enron, the Catholic priests who sexually abused young boys in their congregations, or the person in the ministry who has fallen morally, when accountability is missing, the fallen nature of humanity becomes more apparent and is hurtful to others and to the kingdom of God. For next-level influence to be maintained, accountability must be in place. Consider the following lessons on next-level influence.

1. Accountability Is a Sign of Strength, Not Weakness

Admitting a need for accountability shows the strength of a person's character. Next-level influence demands accountability. No one, no matter his or her position, is beyond the need for accountability. The greater the accountability, the greater the influence. Accountability means making yourself responsible to certain people or groups concerning your actions and attitudes. It is something every person can submit to by a simple choice. From the ministry to the corporate scene, from punching the time clock to working at home, accountability is necessary.

Researchers at Michigan State University discovered that "Ninety-seven percent of the dieters who bet someone they could stick to a weight-loss plan for six months actually succeeded in their pursuit. Conversely, over eighty percent of those who didn't make such bets failed to stay with the dieting regimen. For these dieters, accountability gave them nearly a four-to-one edge toward success."[2]

Obviously I am not suggesting making a bet with some-one, but this study does prove the strength of accountability to another person. Without accountability, vulnerability is heightened. Those in ministry who have morally fallen have most often lacked a system of accountability. Billy Graham has stayed above reproach because he first determined to place himself under accountability to God. But he has also placed himself under accountability to a board of directors and the man who traveled with him all over the world, T. W. Wilson.

No one is beyond the need for another person to whom to be accountable. We never get so big, so successful, and so busy that we can put this need aside. In fact, the more we attempt to do for God, the greater our need for accountability.

2. Choose Accountability Partners Wisely

Next-level influencers seek accountability with people who are modeling that which they desire to become. They choose wisely, prayerfully, and carefully those to whom they will be accountable. It is important that the one or group to whom you will be accountable will ask you the hard questions and be willing to say some hard things to you if necessary.

Accountability refuses to skip the hard questions. If we know that someone is going to ask us the hard questions about what we have done, where we have been, what we have watched, what we have listened to, and what we have thought, we are more inclined to do what is right. Those who always agree with us and don't challenge us are doing us no favor. They may avoid an uncomfortable conversation, but their silence puts us in a vulnerable position.

In accountability relationships, hard questions include: "Have you been inappropriate in any way with a person of the opposite sex?" "Have you daily been in the Bible and prayer?" "Have all of your financial dealings been above reproach?" "Have you viewed any sexually explicit material?" "Have you made spending time with your family a priority?" and "Have you lied about any of these questions?"[3] Those to whom you are accountable should be those who will make it their purpose to encourage rather than discourage you and to build you up spiritually, not drag you down. Faithfulness to a regular time of meeting is also necessary.

An accountability partner is always a person of the same sex. In addition, it needs to be someone (or a group of people) who can be called at a moment's notice to seek prayer, advice, and encouragement. Billy Graham could call T. W. anytime, day or night. Mr. Graham could tell T. W., "I'll pick you up in 15 minutes; we are going on a trip." T. W. kept a suitcase ready at all times.

3. Protecting Your Testimony

Next-level influence is protected through accountability. It becomes the armor by which one's testimony is protected. That is why the Billy Graham Evangelistic Association has been so successful. Their testimony is impeccable. They have put certain safeguards in place to ensure high accountability and maintain a testimony beyond reproach.

The Modesto Manifesto has become a legendary document. In November 1948 in Modesto, California, Billy Graham met with his co-workers and friends George Beverly Shea, Grady Wilson, and Cliff Barrows to determine the most common criticisms of evangelists and how they should organize their own meetings so that they would be above reproach.

Among the points agreed upon were that the Graham team would: "avoid even any appearance of financial abuse, exercise extreme care to avoid even the appearance of any sexual impropriety (from that point on, Graham made it a point not to travel, meet or eat alone with any woman other than his wife, Ruth), to cooperate with any local churches that were willing to participate in a united evangelism effort, and to be honest and reliable in their publicity and reporting of results."[4]

This manifesto was developed prior to T. W. Wilson joining the team; however, those accountability principles continued throughout his involvement in the ministry. When other people know we are accountable, that alone bolsters our testimony. T. W.'s daughter, Sally Pereira, said, "When I worked at the Montreat office, Mr. Graham's response to criticism was to ask us on the staff to pray that we would never be guilty of what they were accusing him of. He prayed rather than lashing out at unfair critics."

4. Accountability Has Great Benefits

Accountability brings with it not only responsibility but also wonderful blessings. Being accountable to another person or a group of people helps us to walk the straight and narrow. Accountability makes us more successful and effective because we know we will answer to someone for what we say and do.

A certain motivation comes within an accountability relationship. An inner joy results from knowing that someone cares enough about us to make it his or her responsibility to make us the best we can be. That's what Billy Graham had in T. W. Wilson—someone whose goal in life was to make him the best he could be, with no personal ambition getting in the way.

Accountability also helps us to keep in focus our mission in life. Through the years, T. W. kept written goals and "to do" lists. Truman Brown notes, "Psychologists have discovered that commitment to a written goal is three times as high as a commitment to a goal that we have only in our head."[5] Highly accountable people often have written goals with a view toward next-level influence. Those written goals become our prayer list and a focus for our faith.

Accountability encourages us to avoid unwise and hasty decisions. When a person has experienced success in any area of leadership, letting down his or her spiritual and emotional guard becomes easier. Accountability helps detect any personal weaknesses or underlying faults and helps prevent that person from falling into temptation as a result of failing to confront those vulnerabilities.

5. Be Accountable First

Before you allow someone to be accountable to you, you first must be accountable. If you are not, pride can easily get in the way. This means we must make ourselves accountable to God for our thoughts and actions, which is encouraged when we are accountable to another person or persons on a regular basis. We cannot expect others to be accountable to us if we have little if any accountability in our own lives.

The following serves as a good example of a lack of personal accountability. On March 10, 2004, the U.S. House of Representatives passed a measure known as the "cheeseburger bill." The bill is designed to protect the fast food industry from potential lawsuits filed by overweight customers. Caesar Barber, age fifty-six, pointed the finger at McDonald's, Wendy's, Kentucky Fried Chicken, and Burger King for his two heart attacks, diabetes, and weight problem. Gregory Rhymes, a fifteen-year-old high school student, joined his mother in blaming fast food restaurants for his obesity. Rhymes's mother stood before a judge and stated, "I always believed McDonald's was healthy for my son." Gregory weighs nearly four hundred pounds. The purpose of the "cheeseburger bill" is to stop these kinds of lawsuits.[6] We are responsible for our own actions.

We should take the initiative because of our own accountability to God and choose people to whom we will be accountable. Personal accountability to God promotes accountability to another person or a group. How? We realize that we need the encouragement and discernment of other people when we make ourselves responsible to obey God in every area of our lives. Our enemy will not allow us to remain committed to God and sit idly by without an attack. We need someone with whom we can pray, share our hearts, seek advice, confess our failures, and vent our frustrations, even when we are frustrated or disillusioned about doing the right thing.

A headline in the *Chicago Tribune* read, "Sober Companions Shadow the Stars." The article says that movie companies or concert promoters sometimes assign "sober companions" to movie and rock stars who have drug or alcohol problems to guard their investments. They want to be sure a move or concert isn't scuttled by an out-of-control star. Also known as "minders" or "clean-living assistants," these folks stick to the stars like glue, making sure they are never alone or accessible to those who might slip them drugs or drink. One sober companion, Tim Tankosic, explains, "The point is to be a rock, a friendly face, a reminder of recovery, a safe person."

The article explains, "On a typical movie location, Tankosic lives with the celebrity in a home far from the hotel that houses the rest of the cast and crew. In the morning, he rises with the star and they meditate together. After breakfast, he accompanies the star to the set, and then to a support group meeting. During off-hours, Tankosic said, he tried to make sure the star has fun, although he steers him or her clear of 'slippery places'—any locale where drugs or alcohol are available." Another "minder" said discretion is a critical part of the job.[7]

In one sense we all need "clean-living assistants," those people who are passionately committed to holding us accountable to do the right thing. To be certain, Christians possess the Holy Spirit, who convicts us when we are not living clean lives, but we also need people whom God can use to encourage us to stay on the right path. God wants us to enjoy life, and that only happens within the parameters of his will.

Next-level influencers possess common characteristics that help them become more accountable:

+ a right relationship with God
+ a daily commitment to reading and applying God's Word
+ a mind that has been cleansed through repentance of its sinful thoughts
+ a habit of worship, both privately and corporately
+ a continual choice to forgive

+ a total obedience to the will of God as revealed in the Word of God
+ a right relationship with one's spouse and family
+ a passion for purity
+ a commitment to following through
+ a marriage to the truth

These characteristics were evident in T. W. Wilson's life. The character traits listed become standards by which we should measure our effectiveness as people of influence. Personal accountability goals encourage us to do the right thing.

11

No Room for Wimps

Next-Level Influencers Have Courage

Sometimes doing the right thing means taking a difficult stand. Unfortunately, political correctness has taken tolerance to new unbiblical heights. Mediocrity is content with not rocking the boat. When courage is called for, Christians cannot just sit idly by. We need to do something—to act, to be proactive. We often hear the slang term "wimp" applied to those who lack courage. A wimp, by definition, is one who will not stand up for what he or she believes in. Wimps have an opinion, but no comment.

T. W. Wilson was no wimp. The man behind Billy Graham was virtually unafraid. He did, however, fear God. Fearing God helps us overcome our fear of people or circumstances. In every sense of the term, T. W. was a man's man. When he knew something was right, he stood up and spoke up for it, no matter what the cost.

His towering presence combined with his gigantic personality made him an impressive man. He was often called a "gentle giant." It was a fitting term, describing his heart and his size. T was an imposing figure, every bit as commanding a presence as Mr. Graham himself. In his latter years, he looked like a retired heavyweight boxer, still in good physical shape.

Billy Graham described his buddy during his pre-salvation days: "Thomas Walter, called T. W. by everybody, a big fellow who could be pretty rough. I would not call him a bully, at least not to his face, but I could safely describe him as burly. T. W. could certainly have had a job as a bouncer!"[1]

In a day when men are asking, "What does it really mean to be a man?" T. W.'s life clearly answered that question. He was said to have had an "iron fist with a silk glove." His courage and manliness could manifest itself even in ministry. The apostle Paul gives us the principles of courage: "Be on the alert, stand firm in the faith, act like men, be strong. Let all that you do be done in love" (1 Cor. 16:13–14). That certainly depicts T. W. Wilson.

Once an intruder came into the Graham team's Montreat office and refused to leave. T. W. overheard the conversation and asked the man to leave the office. When he didn't, T. W. took him by the nape of the neck and firmly handled the problem. He was not intimidated by anyone. Karlene Shea commented, "When there is a crisis, he knows what to do."

T. W.'s friend and former groundskeeper for the Montreat office, Homer Burgin, said of T. W., "The only way I can describe him is to say first of all he is a Christian, a real man of God. He is also a man's man, an upright, thoughtful man who doesn't believe in any nonsense. He's not a wimp; he stands up for what is right, and let me tell you if it's wrong, he stands up against it."

Dr. Stephen Olford related an experience he had at a crusade with T. W.: "I remember sitting with him on a crusade platform. There had been some stupid attempt on Billy's life. I said to T. W., 'How are you facing this?' He said, 'There isn't one split second he is out of my vision.'"

This gentle man could become a giant to contend with when his friend Billy Graham's life was threatened or when his family and friends had been harassed.

Hell Hole Swamp

During his younger days, T. W. preached a two-week revival at a place called Hell Hole Swamp, South Carolina. With the experience he had there, Mary Helen commented, "The place lived up to its name." During one service at that country church, two men were outside cussing and trying to break up the meeting. T. W. asked the head deacon to try to stop the men, but he just shook his head no. T. W. recalled, "And of course, at that time, I knew more about fightin' than I did about preaching anyway. When I saw that he wasn't going to do anything, I went to the back, and there were about three steps to the ground, and when I looked at the man doing the disrupting, he just smiled at me like I was a poodle dog. I took off my jacket and rolled up my sleeves. I jumped down the steps and went over to one fellow, and I socked him and knocked him cold with one lick. Knocked him cold. I turned to the other fellow, and I said, 'Look here, this is God Almighty's house, and we're not going to let the devil interrupt. You get away from here or I'll give you some of the same stuff.' He dragged him off in his old brogans.

"That's where it got around,'This Fightin' Baptist Preacher . . .' That was my title . . . 'The Fightin' Baptist Preacher.'"

The story continues in the Hell Hole Swamp saga. A friend named Henry Schum was with T. W. They were staying in the home of one of the members of the church. A man pulled up and got out of his truck carrying a shotgun, saying, as T. W. tells it, "'Where is that preacher?' He was using the worst foul language possible. He came around the corner and said, 'I'm going to kill that preacher.'"

The man was mad because his brother had gotten converted in the meeting. His brother was with him in the truck and forcefully took the gun out of the man's hand. T. W. went outside. He recalled: "I was stronger and bigger than this man. I looked at him and said, 'Joe, I haven't done a thing in the world to you. You know you were a coward to bring a gun. I could whip you; I'm a better man than you are and you know it. But I'm not going to touch you. I'm going to pray for you. God have mercy on you.'"

Standing Up for What Is Right

While pastoring at Grandview Baptist Church in Dothan, Alabama, the Wilsons had a maid named Mildred. She was like one of their family. Jim Wilson recalls a story about her family: "I was young when all of this took place. Mildred's dad had borrowed some money from a businessman in town. He was a loan shark, probably getting 100 percent interest. He was a bad man. Well, Mildred came to work one day and she was upset and crying and said to T. W., 'My daddy was paid a visit at three o'clock in the morning.'

"Well, that just incensed my daddy. He said, 'Is he coming back tonight? I'll be at your house.' So Daddy went over to the house and he stayed on the couch at Mildred Robinson's house. It was a little house in the poor part of town. Sure enough, in the middle of the night, there was a 'bang, bang, bang' on the door and a big guy was outside. He was shocked out of his mind to see my dad. He didn't know my dad, but Daddy has always been a big guy and he was strong.

"He walked out there and he said, 'What in the world do you think you are doing out here at three o'clock in the morning, harassing these people? I know who you work for, and you can tell your boss that I'll be at his office at eight o'clock in the morning. And if you come back here, you'll have to deal with me.'

"So he went down there at eight o'clock the next morning. He knew that man because he lived not far from us and he drove a certain kind of car—I think it was a Cadillac. My dad saw it outside of his place of business. He walked in, and there were several people in the waiting room, and the lady behind the receptionist desk said, 'May I help you, sir?' He said, 'I'm here to see your boss; we had an appointment at eight o'clock.' She said, 'Who may I say is calling?' 'The Reverend T. W. Wilson.' She said, 'I'm sorry, he has stepped out.'

"Daddy said, 'No ma'am. I see his car right out there. I don't blame him for not wanting to see me.' He began to speak in front of the whole room of people. He told them, 'He's a crook. Folks, I wouldn't do business with this man.' He told all of them what had happened the night before. He said, 'Do you want him banging on your door at three o'clock in the morning?'

"Well, about that time the door opened, and the man came out and said, 'Come on in, preacher.' And then Daddy said, 'No, I think you've heard what I have to say.' And he said, 'If I come in there, I'm afraid of what I might do to you. So, I'm not going to come in there. But I want to say to you, you will not harass Mr. Robinson any more; if you do, you're going to have to deal with me. Do you understand that?' They left Mr. Robinson alone, and he paid his money back to the man at no interest."

Another incident that demonstrated T. W.'s willingness to stand up for what is right came when another evangelist accused Catholics of not being Christians. T. W. Wilson observed that the popular television evangelist was "absolutely wrong" in his insistence that Catholics are not Christians in the eyes of God. "A number of doctrines they teach," Wilson said, "we don't subscribe to, nor would we ever. But to say that they are not Christians—man alive! Anybody who receives Jesus Christ as their Lord and Savior is converted. They're born again! I believe the pope is a converted man. I believe a lot of these wonderful Catholics are Christians."[2]

The Power of Courage

Influence doesn't come from cowardice. Next-level influence demands courage. John McCain says in his book *Why Courage Matters*, "Courage is not the absence of fear, but the capacity for action despite our fears."[3] Courage and conviction show the world that we are serious about the Christian message. When people see that we are willing to stand up for what we believe, they will be more open to that message. To be a leader within the church, within an organization, or in any other setting, courage makes the difference.

To a nervous and unsure Joshua taking the mantle from Moses, God said,

> Only be strong and very courageous; be careful to do according to all the law which Moses My servant commanded you; do not turn from it to the right or to the left, so that you may have success wherever you go. This book of the law shall not depart from your mouth, but you shall meditate on it day and night, so that you may be careful to do according to all that is written in it; for then you will make your way prosperous, and then you will have success. Have I not commanded you? Be strong and courageous! Do not tremble or be dismayed, for the LORD your God is with you wherever you go.

> Joshua 1:7–11

Consider the following lessons on next-level influence.

1. Learn How to Have Courage

Next-level influence involves courage. It is a learned attitude of life. Courage refuses to back down when taking a stand is necessary. Courage refuses to keep quiet when speaking up is necessary. Courage refuses to look the other direction when confrontation is necessary. Ralph Waldo Emerson wrote, "Whatever you do, you need courage. Whatever course you decide upon, there is always someone to tell you that you are wrong. There are always difficulties arising that tempt you to believe your critics are right. To map out a course of action and follow it to an end requires some of the same courage that a soldier needs. Peace has its victories, but it takes brave men and women to win them."[4] Courage begins when one's commitment to God and his Word is stronger than his or her fears.

A next-level influencer understands that without courage there will be no influence. Robert Kennedy said, "Few will have the greatness to bend history itself, but each of us can work to change a small portion of events. . . . It is from numberless acts of courage and belief that human history is shaped."[5] Someone who has courage is almost always influential. We think of Rosa Parks refusing to give up her seat on the bus and the young man in Tiananmen Square who stood in front of those oncoming tanks. Just one courageous act can bring influence and change.

John Wesley said, "Give me a hundred men who fear nothing but sin, and desire nothing but God, and I will shake the world. I care not a straw whether they be clergymen or laymen; and such alone will overthrow the kingdom of Satan and build up the Kingdom of God on earth."[6]

2. Face Fears

Courage does not imply that next-level influencers never have fear. They do, but they admit it and still go on. The next-level influencer claims verses such as: "The LORD is my light and my salvation; Whom shall I fear?" (Ps. 27:1); "Do not be afraid any longer, only believe" (Luke 8:50); "Jesus spoke to them saying, 'Take courage, it is I; do not be afraid.'" (Matt. 14:27); and "Do not fear, for I am with you" (Isa. 44:10). The beginning point of facing fear is fearing God. John Witherspoon wrote, "It is only the fear of God that can deliver us from the fear of men."[7]

3. Stand Up for What Is Right

Next-level influencers stand up for what is right. They allow no compromising of convictions. Those who stand up for what they believe, in the Spirit of Christ, have great influence on others. This includes standing with those who are right and standing up for those who are being abused in any way.

People who will take a stand are somehow refreshing and attractive. The great reformer Martin Luther stood on the biblical teaching of justification by faith and faced the Catholic hierarchy at the Diet of Worms on April 18, 1521. His famous words still ring in our ears: "Here I stand. I can do no other. God help me. Amen!"[8] T. W. Wilson refused to be silent when he needed to speak up. That has influenced many throughout his ministry. People simply respect courage.

In 1934, Adolf Hitler summoned German church leaders to his Berlin office to berate them for insufficiently supporting his programs. Pastor Martin Niemoller explained that he was concerned only for the welfare of the church and of the German people. Hitler snapped, "You confine yourself to the church. I'll take care of the German people." Niemoller replied, "You said that 'I will take care of the German people.' But we too, as Christians and churchmen, have a responsibility toward the German people. That responsibility was entrusted to us by God, and neither you nor anyone in this world has the power to take it from us."

Hitler listened in silence, but that evening his Gestapo raided Niemoller's rectory, and a few days later a bomb exploded in his church. During the months and years following, Niemoller was closely watched by the secret police, and in June 1937 he preached these words to his church: "We have no more thought of using our own powers to escape the arm of the authorities than had the apostles of old. We must obey God rather than man." He was soon arrested and placed in solitary confinement.

He was imprisoned for eight years by Hitler. He spent time in prisons and concentration camps, including Dachau. Hitler realized that if Niemoller could be persuaded to join his cause, much opposition would collapse. So Hitler sent a former friend of Niemoller's to visit him, a friend who supported the Nazis. Seeing Niemoller in his cell, the onetime friend said, "Martin, Martin! Why are you here?" Niemoller replied, "My friend! Why are you not here?"[9]

On September 11, 2001, on board the hijacked jumbo jet possibly on a mission to attack the White House, a Christian named Todd Beamer determined to act. His courageous words "Let's roll" became the battle cry that averted a further terrorist attack on one of America's landmarks.

John, writing in the book of Revelation, said of this kind of courage, "they did not love their life even when faced with death" (Rev. 12:11). As we look back on Christian history, those who have had the greatest influence upon the world have been those who faced their fears and dared to stand up for Christ.

4. Confront When Necessary

Next-level influencers confront when necessary. They aren't constantly looking for a confrontation but will not hesitate when one is required. Francis Schaeffer said, "Truth carries with it confrontation. Truth demands confrontation; loving confrontation, but confrontation nevertheless. If our reflex action is always accommodation regardless of the centrality of the truth involved, there is something wrong."[10] Confrontation often has a negative connotation, but biblical confrontation, done in love, can be the greatest platform for change and influence.

Jesus taught us to confront lovingly: "first take the log out of your own eye, and then you will see clearly to take the speck out of your brother's eye" (Matt. 7:5). "If your brother sins, go and show him his fault in private; if he listens to you, you have won your brother" (Matt. 18:15). Jesus also sets out a process of continued confrontation if the initial confrontation is refused.

A person may not realize he or she is doing something wrong until confronted. At times people have blind spots, not realizing how what they are doing is being perceived. Jesus confronted those who were cruel or abusive to others. Confrontation is the intentional intervention within a situation with the purpose of trying to set things right and change what is wrong.

In his powerful little book *Am I Making Myself Clear?* Terry Felber lists eight foundational principles of confrontation:

1. Anything and everything can be worked out.
2. Deal with the issues at hand, then forgive and forget.
3. Keep a low tone of voice and speak slowly.
4. Depersonalize everything.
5. There are two sides to every story.
6. Ask for forgiveness. Even if you believe you were right and the other person was wrong in a disagreement, you can certainly say with sincerity, "I'm sorry if I upset you. That was never my intention."
7. Never discuss issues of potential conflict on the phone.
8. Never talk about anything important when you're tired.[11]

The next-level influencer lives by such commonsense rules in choosing when to confront.

5. Resolve Conflicts

Next-level influencers seek to solve conflicts. Think about those people who are peacemakers based on truth and love, not on peace at the price of compromising on biblical convictions. They have a real impact. Jesus said, "Blessed are the peacemakers, for they shall be called sons of God" (Matt. 5:9).

Resolving a conflict has immediate results. Studies demonstrate that 70 percent of complaining customers will continue doing business with an organization that favorably resolves their problem. Loyalty jumps to 95 percent if the situation is resolved immediately.[12] Next-level influencers are forgivers. They choose to give up their right to hurt someone who hurts them. People who choose to forgive have great influence on not only those they forgive but others as well. This models the teaching of Jesus Christ to others. Our forgiving others gives credibility to the faith we claim to possess. T. W. Wilson refused to hold a grudge. He chose to love those with whom he had disagreements. He followed what Stephen Covey teaches in his book *The Seven Habits of Highly Effective People*: "to seek first to understand and then to be understood. People do not listen with the intent to understand; they listen with the intent to reply. They're either speaking or preparing to speak. That's the case with so many of us. We're filled with our own rightness, our autobiography. We want to be understood. Our conversations become collective monologues, and we never really understand what's going on inside another human being."[13]

Perhaps this was the key to T. W.'s influence on others. Although he communicated his opinion, he did so with a nonjudgmental attitude. While he stood strong on what he believed, people didn't get the feeling that he was condescending. The truth can be shared without making another person an enemy. When we know a person's perspective, we are in a greater position to influence him or her.

12

What Character Looks Like

Next-Level Influencers Have Integrity

Character has been defined as choosing to do the right thing in any situation, whether or not anyone sees you doing it. It's what you do in the dark. Doing what is right becomes the driving force of a person of character. The Greek word *character* means "to cut," or to engrave. "It is different from a pencil mark that can be erased or a pen that can be eliminated with Wite-Out. It is something that is cut or engraved and cannot be rubbed out."[1]

T. W. Wilson personified character and integrity. His words and life matched. He could be trusted with anything. Dependability was his hallmark. He shared the truth in love, yet when firmness was called for, he gave no thought of what it would cost him personally. That was what influenced so many people—people from all walks of life, all ages, and all socio-economic

169

backgrounds. It is what Billy Graham saw in T at an early age. One of the character-revealing statements T. W. made with passion was: "How you pay your bills is more important than anything else. Talk about Jesus after you have paid your bills."

Jimmy Draper, president of LifeWay Christian Resources and a close friend of the Wilsons, said of T. W., "He never seemed in a hurry. He was unpretentious. You never thought you were talking to an important person, yet he was the one person who had access to Billy."

T. W. recounted, "Years ago a preacher said, 'God almighty wouldn't let an honest man starve if he had to put the angels on half rations for twelve months.'" Another "T-ism" is: "If I was going to be a ditch digger, it would be straight and squared." T. W. always looked straight into your eyes as if looking into your soul.

Billy Graham relates a story from their Fuller Brush sales days:

> One day, T. W. overdid it. He had studied the sales manual backward and forward, and the idea got into his mind that a certain bristle comb was made of bear hair that had been bleached. At one house he launched into his usual talk: "Now if you'll just look at this. No wonder so many movie stars use this particular bristle comb. Notice the alternate rows of bristles. This brush is made out of the best boar-bear bristles that money can buy." "Excuse me," she interrupted. "Did you say 'boar-bear'? I thought a boar was a hog." "Oh, yes, there's a boar-hog, but these bristles are boar-bear, from Russia." To T. W.'s credit, he went to the local library later that afternoon to look up boar-bear. Of course, he couldn't find it.

When he went back to deliver the brush, he confessed to the woman. "I was wrong. You don't even have to buy that brush you ordered. I don't know what made me say what I did, but you're right: a boar is a hog. It must have been the bleaching process that threw me off." Her reply taught him something that all of us tried to remember after that. "Young man," she said, "because you are honest, I want to buy a couple more of your bristle combs."[2]

Don Bailey, retired communications director for the Billy Graham Evangelistic Association and close friend of T. W., said of T. W., "Truthfulness, character, and honesty immediately come to mind. You never had to wonder where you stood with T. W. He would tell you pretty quickly. From shining Billy's shoes to picking out his ties, T. W. contributed to Billy's being on the Best-Dressed Man in America list, although that was not T. W.'s nor Billy's motive. They both spoke the same language, they understood each other, they grew up together, they've known each other all their lives and know their families.

"From that standpoint they trusted each other. Billy trusts T. W. implicitly. He could say exactly what he thought to Billy. T knew about his schedule, where he needed to be, the mundane, his luggage—all of these things, T did in such a Christlike spirit. He put aside his own needs to meet Billy's needs."

Dr. Stephen Olford describes T. W. in his famous alliterative style: "I would describe T. W. in three words: *selflessness, steadfastness,* and *sacrificial.* He was selfless in that he always thought of Billy and his needs first. He was steadfast in that he stuck to it. He got the job done. He was sacrificial in that he sacrificed an entire ministry of public preaching and pastoring in order to stand by Billy." These are all good character qualities.

Humility Is Powerful

T. W. Wilson exemplified humility in all his dealings with people. He found no dishonor in being a behind-the-scenes person. T was no respecter of persons. Whether he was with a president or a prisoner, T. W. was the same. His humility gave him an attractive transparency, a quality demonstrated in Jesus. His daughter, Sally, while retrieving something for her dad in his Montreat office, noticed a stack of pictures in T. W.'s desk drawer. They were pictures of T. W. with presidents and dignitaries. When asked about it, T. W. said, "I got under conviction about having them up, so I put them in a desk drawer under things." That humility was not to impress people—it was genuine.

T. W. said of his official title in the organization: "Years ago Dr. Graham wanted to give me a highfalutin sounding title, and I said, 'Billy, I have enough responsibilities as it is. Just let me be one of your associates.' I have had a combination of responsibilities with radio stations, the Montreat office as manager, World Wide Publications, and some other things, but I've never sought a title. I just considered it a great privilege to be Associate Evangelist and travel companion with my boyhood friend, who grew up under the leadership of the Holy Spirit to be a great evangelist."

Glenn Wilcox recalled this exchange with T. W.: "[I said,] 'T, the most amazing thing about you is that you're the number two man, and when you all travel the news reporters, the photographers say, "T. W., would you step over here? I want to take a picture of the Queen and Billy," or Senator so-and-so and Billy, or President such-and-such and Billy. You're never in the pictures. You orchestrate it, you do all the work; you go back and write letters for Billy to help him. You do all this stuff and get no credit. I don't see your name up there anywhere.' T said to me, 'Glenn, it's more important to be in God's will than to have your name up there in a place of prominence.'"

Luis Palau said of T. W.: "One thing about him is his humility. Though he looks so tall and aggressive when you don't know him, when you think that he sublimated his calling as a preacher . . . those who have heard him preach said that he is very good, but he sublimated it just to help Billy do his job." T. W. always said, "There's no limit to what you can do if you don't care who gets the credit."

Giving Attention to the Little Things

Once when Julie Eisenhower was visiting with the Grahams in Montreat, she and Ruth were driving up the hill to their house. Julie was sitting on the microphone of the CB radio. You could hear everything they were saying. Julie asked Ruth about Grady. Ruth said, "Grady is so much fun with his jokes and stories." Then Julie said, "What about T. W.?" Ruth responded, "If you want something done, go to T. W."

Once Billy gave T a list of twelve things to do. T did them immediately, and the next morning Billy couldn't believe he had done them so fast. Billy told him, "I meant for you to do them the rest of the week."

The details T. W. managed included handling all of Mr. Graham's itinerary when traveling anywhere in the world—booking the hotel, booking the flight, getting maps of where they were going, securing transportation, leaving behind numbers to get in touch with them (in the days before cell phones), and figuring out the monetary exchange if traveling in a different country. With T. W. around, Mr. Graham didn't have to worry about the details. T. W. helped Billy with his clothes, made sure his shoes were shined, ordered his meals, and carried his luggage.

Dr. Stephen Olford shares this insight: "I traveled with Billy, and T. W. would think through Billy's wardrobe, passports, official papers, so that he never had to think about a thing or say a word. T. W. cleared the red tape ahead of time. He drew attention to Billy, never to himself. He would never sympathize with Billy. He monitored his pills, his medicines, and his vitamins each day. He had a way of bringing peace to Billy concerning his physical ailments like no one else."

T. W. could get things done. At a London crusade in 1986, T. W. told one of Mr. Graham's assistants that Billy wanted something. The man responded with, "It can't be done." T. W. said, "Why can't it be done?" The man said, "Well, it's just never been done before." T said, "Then you can be the first one to do it." The man turned and walked off and got it done.

Jim Wilson tells this story about how important details were to his dad: "There were many dignitaries that came in to meet Billy before a crusade. Billy, bless his heart, can't remember everything he says to everybody. He will make promises to people, and he intends to keep every one of them, but he forgets. He's human. Well, my dad was over there with a little note pad, and he would write down the name of the person and what Billy had promised to do for him or send him. Immediately Daddy would follow up. This protected Billy's integrity."

World Medical Missions

Glenn Wilcox's father was in the hospital in Boone, North Carolina, and had been diagnosed with cancer. He was in his seventies, and surgery would not be possible. The man was extremely discouraged and refused to eat. Glenn asked T. W. if he would go see him and attempt to get him to eat.

T. W. walked into the room to visit Herman Wilcox just as they were bringing his lunch. Herman said to the nurse, "I don't want it and I won't eat it; take it away." T said, "Now, Mr. Herman, you've got to eat to live, and you're going to eat this, and we're going to pray for you before you eat it, and you'll like it." T. W. prayed, Mr. Herman ate, and the doctor, Richard Furman, was amazed.

But this wasn't the end of the story. Dr. Furman was greatly impressed by T. W.'s personality and character. Later God would place upon this Dr. Furman's heart to begin an organization that would touch the world with the love of God. T. W. was invited to a meeting with Dr. Furman. There were eighteen inches of snow on the ground, but T. W.'s tenacity took over. "I have a Jeep, and I'm going to get to that meeting," he said. That night at their meeting, World Medical Missions was birthed.

A Number One Man in a Number Two Position

T. W. has been called "the invisible man," "the servant's servant," "man in the shadows," and "a number one man in a number two position." He has been called the second fiddle—not in the sense of not being as significant to God but in the sense of not being the out-front person. Richard Bewes, Rector of All Souls' Church, Langham Place, in London, said of T. W., "The remarkable thing about T. W. is that he is greatly smitten with the fact that he is not seen. Sometimes there were times when Billy would go to see some important person, some very important person, and he did not like ever to go alone. He'd say, 'Oh, T, come with me. T, come on . . .' And then T. W. sits out in the lobby while the interview or whatever it is goes on."

Ross Rhoads said, "Nobody ever worked for Billy; he didn't like that word. T. W. and Grady and Cliff and Bev were 'with' him from the beginning. You would always get the impression that nobody was second, third, or fourth." For T. W., it wasn't a matter of prestige; it was a matter of calling.

In describing T. W., Dr. John R. W. Stott quoted the little doggerel, "It takes more grace than I could tell, to play the second fiddle well." Evelyn Freeland, T. W.'s longtime assistant, said, "He was a number one man who was content with a number two position." T. W. realized that there was no higher calling than that of a servant.

Betty Drummond, wife of the late Dr. Lewis Drummond and close friend of the Wilsons, said of T. W., "We forget that God gifts all of us, and we don't have to be the shining light of the parlor, but we can be the 'back hall light.'"

Loyalty

Loyalty describes T. W.'s relationship not only with Billy Graham but with anyone who was his friend. Cliff Barrows echoed this idea: "Billy feels very grateful to God and very indebted to God for T. W.'s life, his commitment, and his loyalty. You never questioned T. W.'s loyalty, either to the Lord or to the one with whom he was working, Billy Graham. It is even more important these days. Loyalty seems to be one of the things that is missing so much in church staffs. The commitment he had has been a real example to all of us."

After Wilson's death the *Asheville Citizen-Times* ran an editorial titled, "T. W. Wilson: The Real Deal." It read in part:

> To sum up a life in a few words spread across newsprint rarely does the individual justice. In this particular case, it's especially true; no amount of printer's ink could do justice to T. W. Wilson, who passed away Thursday [May 24, 2001]. And yet we owe it to him to try.
>
> Wilson was one element in a historic collaboration that included George Beverly Shea and Billy Graham. Graham, of course, needs no introduction. Shea, of course, is known for the golden voice.
>
> Wilson was regarded as the right-hand man that helped form a bond that lasted decades and spanned continents. As a young man Wilson roamed the woods near Charlotte with a young Billy Graham. "T," as he was known to friends, was an ordained Southern Baptist Minister. He graduated from Bob Jones University in 1941, and followed that up with graduate work at the University of Alabama before entering the seminary. His resume includes pastoring several Baptist churches, serving as vice president of Youth for Christ and vice president of Northwestern Schools in Minneapolis. He is well known in WNC for serving as president of Blue Ridge Broadcasting Corp. and spreading the gospel over WFGW-AM in the Swannanoa Valley. His home, in one sense, was in Montreat. In another, it was with the Billy Graham Evangelistic Association and wherever that might take him.
>
> His list of accomplishments was impressive. But two things stand out about T. W. Wilson. Consider that we are in an age

of self-promotion, an age where salesmanship means more than product. An age where scandal seems more the rule than the exception. Consider how long the Graham ministries have been around, and how, despite its high profile, it's hard to think of a tinge of scandal associated with it; it's impossible to think of the phrase "self-promotion" associated with the ministry. There's a reason for that. This group is the real deal.

In an age where the sin of pride (and subsequent fall) has almost seemed mandatory among well-known religious figures and groups, Graham's group has simply marched right along, keeping its focus where it rightfully should be. And there, helping to steer it, feeling no need to bask in the spotlight, was T. W. Wilson. "You have to remember who we are working for," Wilson said. "I believe God has got his hands on Billy. God called me to help him do it."[3]

The Power of Character

Next-level influencers are people of character. In a day when character seems to be eroding at all levels of leadership, Christians who desire to make a difference in their world must have an impeccable character. That is not to say they are perfect, only that they strive always to do what is right. When they fail, they admit it, take responsibility for it, and continue doing what is right. Next-level influencers admit when they have blown it, but they also don't stay down. They get up in the power of a resurrected Savior. Consider the following lessons on next-level influence.

1. Character Forms the Basis for Influence

Next-level influence hinges on character. One bumper sticker had it right: "Live so that the preacher won't have to lie at your funeral."[4] The next-level influencer places character above image, education, money, popularity, or position.

Character is not what you do, although what you do is driven by character. Character is not something you say, although what you say reflects your character. Character is who you are regardless of where you are, when it is, or whose company you are in at the time. It is formed behind the scenes, when no one is watching. Character is the compilation of godly private habits and also the sum of the choices you have made.

Character comes onto the stage during those times when you are facing complex choices, difficult issues, and stressful circumstances. What you did in the behind-the-scenes times is then brought to light. Character refuses to cut corners, take shortcuts, or look for the path of least resistance when it comes to doing what is right. T. W. Wilson said, "When we look at people who have poor character or a poor lifestyle, we lose confidence, we have no real respect for their lack of integrity."

Next-level influencers protect their character at all costs. They keep the highest moral standards possible. Character demands that sin be immediately confessed and that our thought life be constantly under the microscope of God's Word and the Holy Spirit. John R. W. Stott said, "What we are governs how we think, and how we think determines how we act."[5] In his book *Spurgeon on Leadership*, Larry J. Michael says, "Christian leaders, above all, must demonstrate moral character if they expect to exert lasting influence upon their followers. People lose faith in their leaders when their morals are compromised. Spurgeon used the phrase 'greatest power' to describe the influence that a leader could have over his followers. 'Let us aspire to saintliness of spirit and character. I am persuaded that the greatest power we can get over our fellow-men is the power which comes of consecration and holiness.'"[6]

James said it clearly: "Consider it all joy, my brethren, when you encounter various trials, knowing that the testing of your faith produces endurance. And let endurance have its perfect result, so that you may be perfect and complete, lacking in nothing" (James 1:2–4).

2. Humility Is Necessary for God's Favor

Humility has been called "the mother, root, nurse, foundation, and center of all other virtues."[7] Humility brings the favor of God and the promise of promotion from God. The next-level influencer is one who has the favor of God upon him. "Therefore humble yourselves under the mighty hand of God, that He may exalt you at the proper time" (1 Peter 5:6). Jesus said, "Whoever exalts himself shall be humbled; and whoever humbles himself shall be exalted" (Matt. 23:12). Next-level influencers are not overly impressed with themselves, nor are they self-condemning. They have balanced their perspective knowing the deceitfulness of their own hearts and the greatness of our gracious God.

On his way to a reception in his honor, Ulysses S. Grant got caught in a rainstorm. He shared his umbrella with a stranger going to the same reception who did not recognize Grant. "I have never seen Grant," he said, "but I have always thought he was a very much overrated man." "That's my view, also," said Grant.[8]

T. W. Wilson was content to be second, a Jonathan encouraging and helping a David. Vance Havner, a friend of T. W.'s, said, "Blessed are the saints of the second fiddle."[9] T. W. played that position well, and it had a harmonizing effect upon the whole Graham organization. Next-level influencers care more about getting the task accomplished and seeing God get the credit than about having the applause of people.

A. W. Tozer said, "The meek man is not a human mouse afflicted with a sense of his own inferiority. Rather he may be in his moral life as bold as a lion and as strong as Samson; but he has stopped being fooled about himself. He has accepted God's estimate of his own life. He knows he is as weak and helpless as God declared him to be; put paradoxically, he knows at the same time that he is in the sight of God of more importance than angels. In himself, nothing; in God, everything. That is his motto."[10]

3. Pay Attention to Details

"Be great in little things," said Augustine.[11] The next-level influencer pays attention to little things. Doing those little things matters. It is returning the phone call, writing a thank-you note, being on time, or giving your time to someone who can do absolutely nothing for you. In essence, it is keeping your word. Imagine how impressed a person would have been when he got a note, a Bible, a card, or a book from Billy Graham. He had promised it, and he kept his word.

Yet behind him was a note-taker, the detail man, listening to everything Billy promised he would do and then immediately following up on it. T. W. Wilson paid attention to the little things. Next-level influence takes place first behind the scenes, making sure the details are all handled. Influence depends upon it. Attention to the little things builds our integrity with others. Integrity means wholeness, integration. It is integrating what you say with what you do; it is consistency of words and actions, belief and behavior. "The integrity of the upright will guide them" (Prov. 11:3). Or as Roy Zuck put it, "Little things are the hinges on which great results turn."[12]

4. Loyalty Is a Hallmark

Next-level influence requires loyalty. Of first importance is an intense loyalty to Jesus Christ—his message, his teachings, his cause, and his Word. Loyalty to him takes precedence over loyalty to anyone else. Loyalty to one's convictions is also required, as well as loyalty to people, specifically our spouse, our children, our family, and those we call friends. Disloyalty destroys next-level influence.

The English hymn "I Vow to Thee My Country," which was sung both at Princess Diana's wedding and funeral, gives an excellent portrayal of loyalty:

I vow to thee my country, all earthly things above.
Entire and whole and perfect, the service of my love.
The love that asks no questions, the love that stands the test.
That lays upon the altar the dearest and the best.
The love that never falters, the love that pays the price.
The love that makes undaunted the final sacrifice.

And there's another country, I've heard of long ago,
Most dear to them that love her, most great to them that know.
We may not count her armies, we may not see her King,
Her fortress is a faithful heart, her pride is suffering.
And soul by soul and silently, her shining bounds increase,
And her ways are ways of gentleness and all her paths are peace.[13]

One of the greatest examples of loyalty in the Bible is Jonathan's loyalty to David. Samuel tells us his soul was "knit to the soul of David" (1 Sam. 18:1). Jonathan put his own life on the line for David. We see that knitting of souls with T. W. and Billy Graham. An editorial in *Christianity Today* on July 9, 2001, said of T. W., "in the inner circle, he was the trusted soulmate."[14] T's loyalty to Billy Graham is legendary. He believed what Theodore Roosevelt said: "It is better to be faithful than famous."[15] T. W. said, "Dependability is one of the greatest abilities. I guess we've all met people who are vacillating and wishy-washy—one thing to this one and another thing to somebody else. People who are loyal can be relied upon, depended upon."

5. Remain Diligent

The next-level influencer possesses a diligence in all his tasks. He sets out with a determined and enthusiastic spirit to accomplish his assignments. No one ever questions his work ethic. He gets things done. There is no spot of laziness upon him. Paul describes this person as "not lagging behind in diligence, fervent in spirit, serving the Lord" (Rom. 12:11).

Diligence means to approach a task as if you were doing it for Jesus himself. Diligence embodies the "and then some" principle. Next-level influencers don't just do what is necessary; they go beyond what is expected with joy and without complaint. Diligence also means availability, always being willing to do what needs to be done. The writer of Proverbs tells us to watch ants as examples of diligence (Prov. 6:6). The ant is self-motivated; no one has to tell it to get busy. It finds a way to get things done, even seemingly impossible things. The next-level influencer embodies what Paul said in Colossians 3:17: "Whatever you do in word or deed, do all in the name of the Lord Jesus, giving thanks through Him to God the Father."

Herbert V. Prochrow writes in "A Businessman's Prayer,"

Help me, O Lord, to remember that three feet make one yard, sixteen ounces make one pound, four quarts make one gallon, and sixty minutes make one hour. Help me to do business on the square. Make me sympathetic with the fellow who has been broken in the struggle. Keep me from taking an unfair advantage of the weak, or from selling my self-respect for a profit. Blind my eyes to the petty faults of others, but reveal to me my own. And when comes to the sound of low music, the scent of sweet flowers, and the crunch of footsteps on the gravel, make the ceremony short, and the epitaph simply—"Here lies a man . . . one who was of service to others."[16]

That is precisely what a next-level influencer tries to be.

13

FAMILY AND FRIENDS

*Next-Level Influencers
Prioritize Relationships*

T. W. Wilson never met a stranger. Upon meeting him one immediately felt comfortable, like reuniting with an old friend. His warmth and kind disposition quickly invited people into a relationship with him. He passionately loved his family and his friends. Some of his personal relationships may have been possible because of his position with Billy Graham, but they were built and continued through the years because of his personality and his selfless temperament. People were drawn to him like a moth to an open flame. His people skills were second to none. T. W. often introduced people with, "This is one of my dearest and best friends." He meant it. It wasn't just a cliché.

He befriended countless people and helped them financially without anyone ever knowing it. He didn't want credit; he just wanted to be a blessing. Even to those who were critical of him—and there were very few—he demonstrated a love and Christlike spirit.

The late Dr. Roger James, T. W. and Billy's physician, said of T. W., "You can look around his house and see his books and look at his bank account and see where he gives. He is so gracious, so kind, so helpful, and just so positive. You can't help but like to be around him. Even after his stroke, he's still positive." T. W. loved to talk about his brother Grady. He missed him terribly and would often talk about Grady's sense of humor. T. W. loved to share about the time that a man came up to Grady after a crusade and said, "We like you, Brother Grady. You don't give us no doctrine, no nothin.'"

All the children of the Graham team members call the other team members "Uncle." Billy Graham's children call T. W. "Uncle T." And T. W.'s children, Jimmy and Sally, call Mr. Graham "Uncle Billy." The team and their families are a close-knit family who truly love and respect each other.

T. W. had the opportunity to be a second dad to the Graham children. T. W. was very close to Dr. Nelson Bell, Ruth Graham's father. He loved him so much and valued his godly advice. In fact, Mrs. Bell called T. W. one morning and said, "T. W., I think something is wrong with Nelson." T. W. said, "I'll be right there." He greeted Mrs. Bell and walked into the room where Dr. Bell had been sleeping. T. W. looked at him for a minute and then said to Mrs. Bell, "Mrs. Bell, Dr. Bell has gone on to heaven."

Mary Helen

Countless times T. W. said, "There has never been a more blessed man than I am because of my darling Mary Helen." They celebrated their fiftieth anniversary on June 26, 1992. Mary Helen was the faithful, devoted, loving wife and mother who allowed T. W. to have a next-level influence. She never complained about all those times T had to be away from her and the children. She is adored by everyone who meets her. By all accounts, Mary Helen is completely unselfish. She would much rather do something for somebody else or give up something for herself so that somebody else could receive a blessing. She is the epitome of a lady. She feels at home with anyone, including royalty.

On the Wilsons' fiftieth anniversary, Fred and Millie Dienert arranged a great surprise celebration during the Philadelphia crusade. They flew the whole family up to join them. Billy was told at the last minute because those in charge knew he would be so excited that he might let the news slip to T. W. Billy was to arrange to get T. W. to the hotel where the celebration was held. That was different—Billy Graham making sure T. W. got somewhere.

T. W. would often talk about how Mary Helen had stayed behind him with "the stuff" and would be rewarded equally with him. What did he mean by "the stuff"? The answer is found in 1 Samuel 30:24 when King David says, "For who will hearken unto you in this matter? But as his part is that goeth down to the battle, so shall his part be that tarrieth by the stuff: they shall part alike" (KJV). David had defeated the Amalekites and recovered all the spoils. He realized it was the Lord who had won the battle for them. David shared the spoils with those who assisted him in this victory.

T. W.'s feelings toward Mary Helen could be summed up by what King Lemuel said about a virtuous woman in Proverbs 31:10–12: "Who can find a virtuous and capable wife? She is worth more than precious rubies. Her husband can trust her, and she will greatly enrich his life. She will not hinder him but help him all her life" (NLT).

Defeating an Enemy Called Stroke

When T. W. had his stroke, Mary Helen pulled him through. T. W. had been at Wheaton College representing Mr. Graham at the retirement party for Dr. Robert Coleman from the Billy Graham Center at the school. That night T. W. went back to his hotel room. John Akers, another Graham team member, had traveled with him and was staying in another room. That night T. W. had his stroke. He called the front desk but no one answered. He opened the room door, lay down on the bed, and prepared to die. He fell asleep and woke up the next morning feeling almost normal. He never even told John Akers what had happened.

T. W. tells what happened next: "We flew back home together and Mary Helen met me at the airport. We went to a little eating place near the airport. I began to get tired, I asked her to let me look at the mail, and I began to read some of it. I said, 'Darlin', I just don't feel right. I don't know what's the matter with me.' She said, 'Well, let's go home. We'll go through the mail at home.' I got to feeling worse.

"She called a doctor, a longtime friend, a Christian, Dr. Roger James. She told him how I was, and he came out there and he said, 'I think we'd better get him to the hospital.' I didn't take any clothes or anything. They did some kind of tests. He said, 'T, I think you need to stay.' I said, 'I don't want to stay here.' He said, 'I think you'd better stay.'

"The stroke progressed over several days. In the middle of the night when the stroke began to worsen, I felt like the whole world was turned around. I didn't know what in the world was happening. It was about 2:00 a.m. I looked around and all of a sudden, this whole side was dead. I called for a nurse. I told her what I discovered and she said, 'Well, you've had a stroke.'

"And then I was in the middle of it. They had everything hooked up to me. I remember how embarrassed I was because I didn't want any nurse waiting on me."

The stroke affected his short-term memory and his ability to read. Interestingly enough, he could write but not read. He didn't know anyone's names initially. However, he did call Mary Helen "Darling." In a few days he simply wanted to give up because he was so frustrated. That's when Mary Helen pulled him out of it. She looked at him and said, "You are not the same T. W. Wilson I married, because that man was never a quitter." That did it. He willed to live and even started working with a therapist to learn to read again.

Sally shared an incident about her dad and his memory: "I called Daddy and said, 'Daddy, I've got a verse for you from *Daily Light.'* I started saying, 'The Lord is good . . .'. He immediately continued the verse by saying, 'A stronghold in the day of trouble.' Then he added, 'And he is . . . "And he knows those who trust in Him" (Nahum 1:7).' His years of Bible reading had permeated his mind with its truths."

He never complained, not once, about his condition. Quite the opposite, he said the greatest times with the Lord he had ever known had been since the stroke. He daily got up and walked. He worked diligently to learn again. Every morning he and Mary Helen had their devotions by listening to Scripture on tape and then discussing it. He was beating this stroke day by day through prayer, determination, and love for his wife and family.

T. W. would say to Mary Helen, "Darling, come sit on my lap." It was an act of affection they had practiced every day they saw each other. Sally Pereira related this moving event on the last day of his life: "Daddy was especially uneasy that morning. But I remember he called out to Mother and said, 'Mary Helen, I want you to come sit on my lap.' He said, 'Do you ever get tired of me telling you how much I love you? Because I would hate to die and leave you not knowing how much I love you.'" Only two and one-half hours later, T went home to heaven as Mary Helen was driving him to see a friend after they had eaten lunch in Black Mountain. She lives with those precious words in her memory. T. W. died with his boots on. He was going to tell that friend one more time about Jesus.

Family Matters

T said, "Things don't matter, family does." Did he have any regrets about his family and all the traveling he had to do? He shared the following: "Well, I think I should have spent more time, especially in those early days, with my family."

However, he made it up to them in numerous ways. He had a great relationship with all of his grandchildren. Each of them shows great love and respect for their granddaddy. He was their hero. One of his granddaughters, Christy Kurpier, whose son is named after T. W., commented, "He's never said a cross word to me, never been ugly to me. He's always loved me, no matter what. The people who don't know my grandfather don't realize what a far-reaching ministry he has had behind the scenes. He always wanted to be the helpmate, the silent person. Because of the Billy Graham ministry, it has helped keep our lives on course, and Granddaddy had a career with that, and he's had a wonderful life because of that ministry. But he's also added to it, and he's been an integral part that cannot be separated from it."

Carol Anne Hanks, T. W.'s niece, spoke of her undying gratitude for "Uncle T's" influential contribution to her life. Her dad died when she was nine. T. W. and Mary Helen came to get Carol Anne for the summer. He had promised her dad that he would take care of her. Eventually, she and her mother came to live with them for a year. Afterwards, going to the Wilsons' Montreat home became a regular part of her life.

T. W. and Mary Helen introduced Carol Anne to Billie Hanks, a Texas evangelist whose father in the ministry had been Grady Wilson. Carol Anne and Billie were married, and both spent every Christmas with T. W. and Mary Helen.

Carol Anne, recalling her younger days, said of T. W., "I worshipped the ground he walked on. Every single night we had devotions in their little den. One of the things that he has taught me the most—there are many of them, but spiritually—I think is humility. He is the most humble-spirited man that I have ever known. I have never heard him once, no matter what the situation, say an unkind word about anybody for any reason." She further spoke of how Jimmy and Sally were never jealous of sharing their dad and mom. They learned the same warmth and love as their parents possessed.

An Invitation from Billy

A young Billy Graham wrote dozens of letters to his buddy T. W. He signed almost every letter, "Your Pal, Billy." This letter, however, especially warms the heart. It was dated January

19, 1942, and written as Billy Graham was sitting in a class at Wheaton College:

> Dear T. W.,
>
> It was a real joy to hear your voice the other day as it came ringing over the telephone. Immediately, my dull mind went back to other days when we enjoyed fellowship under other conditions.
>
> Also, I was glad to receive your good letter a few days ago and trust that this answer is not too late for your convenience.
>
> I think that the idea of marriage is a good one; it is on my mind as usual. But if all goes well I hope to be married this summer or fall. I want to ask you to be the <u>best man in our wedding</u>. Of all the friends I have ever had, I hold you nearest to my heart. As I have seen you grow in the grace and knowledge of our Lord Jesus, I have rejoiced with you at every step and continue to pray that you might be used of Him in these days of darkness. Our friendship has had many interruptions over the years but I still count you my very best friend and would be disappointed if you were not able to accept my invitation to be best man.
>
> Your Pal,
> Billy[1]

T. W.'s Homegoing Service

T. W. would often say, "Life is short, even at its longest." On May 28, 2001, at the First Baptist Church of Swannanoa, North Carolina, his family had a celebratory homegoing service for him. The church was filled with people, well known and not so well known, whom T. W.'s life had touched. To T. W. there was no difference between the two. His pal Billy Graham gave the eulogy. Mr. Graham had been at the Mayo Clinic in Jacksonville, Florida, for several weeks, but he refused to miss T. W.'s funeral. He opened his Bible to 1 Chronicles 4:10 and made an insightful comparison between the man Jabez and T. W. Wilson:

> The first petition in the prayer of Jabez is, "Oh, bless me indeed." God wonderfully blessed T. W. with a wonderful and positive, happy personality that kept him smiling. As we talked over the last few weeks he said to me, "Billy, Romans 8:28 is still in the Bible." God blessed him with a wonderful family and a host of friends around the world.
>
> The second petition in the prayer of Jabez is, "Enlarge my territory," give me more to do in a greater way than I am doing now. He enlarged T. W.'s ministry many times, as pastor of a small Baptist church in Alabama, and from there God allowed him to travel to many parts of the world and win people to Christ. Many years ago he put together a quartet, a group of four men, who traveled in England and Ireland. T. W. helped Cliff Barrows, George Beverly Shea, Grady Wilson, and me in the work of evangelism. He encouraged us and helped us. The territory that God had given to us was a part of T. W.'s territory for which we are grateful.
>
> The third petition in the prayer of Jabez is that "God's hand would be upon him." There never was any doubt in my mind that God's hand was on T. W. God gave him a variety of gifts, gifts in the service of the Lord and evangelism. Whoever he came in contact with, he talked to them about the Lord. He led people to Christ in quiet and personal ways. In addition to public preaching, that many didn't know about, he had the gift of helping others. He was a helper and encourager to my own ministry by his dedication and his able assistance for many years.

Fourthly, Jabez prayed that "God would keep him from evil." The Lord answered that kind of prayer for T. W. We all face temptation as we go through life. But I never knew him to yield because God kept him from doing wrong. He knew what it meant to walk with God every day. He read the Bible a great deal. Many times he was called upon to lead in public prayer and I can still hear in my mind some of the great prayers he prayed. But he also made prayer a part of his daily life. I already miss him greatly. His personal friendship to my family and to our organization and to our team of people was a gift to us from God. I join with you in thanking God for T. W.'s life and his faith in our Lord Jesus Christ and to Mary Helen who has been one of the most faithful wives and mothers I have ever known. Also, to Jim and Sally and their families and the legacy he has left behind. My petition to the Lord today is, "God, continue to bless the family of T. W. Wilson and may the life that he lived be a lasting example." God bless you all.[2]

After Mr. Graham finished and T. W.'s favorite hymn, "He Lives," was sung, Don Bailey read a personal response from Dr. Bill Bright. Dr. Bright was too ill to travel to the memorial service. His words demonstrate the wonderful influence T. W. possessed in Bill and Vonette Bright's lives:

T. W. Wilson was one of the most loving, gracious men of whom I have ever known. But the quality that has impressed me most about this man during the more than 50 years of our warm friendship is his humble, serving spirit. He followed the example of our Lord Jesus Christ who he loved and served with all of his heart. God has surrounded me with wonderful young men to help me serve the worldwide staff and ministry of Campus Crusade for Christ. As a part of my mentoring and modeling, I inevitably tell them about T. W. Wilson, who to me was one of the best examples of a servant leader I have ever known. I am confident that Billy Graham would be the first to say that T. W. has greatly enhanced his worldwide ministry. I am equally confident that millions of people will be in heaven because of our big, loving, ever-smiling gracious servant, friend, and brother, Dr. T. W. Wilson.[3]

Franklin Graham offered his personal words at T. W.'s memorial service to thank his "Uncle T" for his love, friendship, counsel, and steady hand. He told the *Asheville Citizen-Times*, "T. W. Wilson gave 100 percent to my father and his ministry. I don't think my father could have gone this far without him."[4]

Another highlight of the service was when George Beverly Shea and Cliff Barrows came to the platform and sang as a duet another of T. W.'s favorite songs. When they sang "How Great Thou Art," there wasn't one person without a tear or a goose bump. Dr. Jerry Pereira, T. W.'s son-in-law and pastor of the church, gave a heart-moving, Christ-exalting message. In 2003, Jerry discovered he had cancer, and he has now joined T. W. in heaven. The service was not only a testimony to T. W.'s great ministry but a testimony to one who placed relationships as the priority of his life.

Since the beginning of research for this book in 2000, many of the wonderful people I had the privilege of meeting have gone home to heaven. What a reunion—Bill Bright, Johnny Cash, Dr. Lewis Drummond, Jerry Pereira, Dr. Stephen Olford, and Dr. Roger James. Grady Wilson is probably still the court jester, now of heaven. T. W. is finally home. We believe when he got there he heard these words, "Well done, thou good and faithful servant."

The Power of Family and Friends

Next-level influencers prioritize relationships with first family and then friends. Through those relationships the world begins to change, one person at a time. T. W. Wilson demonstrated that relationships were his priority—his wife, Mary Helen, first, then his children, his grandchildren, his extended family, the Graham family, and a host of friends. That alone gave him next-level influence. Mother Teresa said, "We are all pencils in the hand of a writing God, who is sending love letters to the world."[5] Consider these lessons of next-level influence.

1. Make Family Your Priority

Next-level influencers put family as the top priority of their lives after their relationship with Jesus Christ. The greatest influence one can have is with his or her family. If one has no next-level influence with family, one will have little, if any, influence outside the family. Patrick Morley made the following observation while talking with his wife: "One evening as we reviewed our calendar and a stack of time-consuming opportunities, the thought came, 'Why not prioritize everything we do on the basis of who's going to be crying at our funeral?' We did it. The results saved our family. This simple question—'Who's going to be crying at our funeral?'—cuts out time wasters with the accuracy of a laser beam. Why should you and I give ourselves to people who don't love us, at the expense of those who do?"[6] This puts in perspective the importance of family.

When we influence our families toward God, we are successful. Julian Lennon, son of John Lennon, said, "I felt he was a hypocrite. Dad could talk about peace and love out loud to the world, but he could never show it to the people who supposedly meant the most to him: his wife and son. How can you talk about peace and love and have a family in bits and pieces—no communication, adultery, divorce? You can't do it, not if you're being true and honest with yourself."[7] People watch our families, our homes. If we have no power to influence our families, how can we expect to influence the world?

2. Build Friendships

Next-level influence involves the building of relationships. This takes time, energy, and some risk. Influence occurs within the boundaries of relationships. Next-level influencers build warm, friendly relationships that push people closer to God. Christianity's greatest influence will not come from television programs, radio spots, newspaper ads, or huge events. It will come as a result of the relationships that we build. Trust is a crucial factor in communicating the gospel. If people are suspicious, they are less inclined to listen to our faith appeal. However, when trust is built and people can see Christianity at work, then they will be more open to hearing about the Christ behind it.

Author Robert D. Putnam in his book *Bowling Alone* calls the building of relationships "social capital." He writes, "The core idea of social capital theory is that social networks have value."[8] To be able to have next-level influence, we must build up our "social capital."

3. A Solid Marriage

If married, a next-level influencer knows that his marriage must be constantly growing and never allowed to stagnate. Alan Loy McGinnis says, "In physics, the law of entropy says that all systems, left unattended, will run down. Unless new energy is pumped in, the organism will disintegrate. Entropy is at work in many areas other than physics. I see it, for instance, when I work with couples whose marriages are in trouble. A marriage will not continue to be good simply because two people love each other, are compatible, and get off to a fine start. To the contrary, marriages left to their own devices tend to wear out, break down, and ultimately disintegrate. This is the law of entropy. So to keep our relationships working, we must constantly pump new energy into them."[9]

A husband and wife make a great team for next-level influence. That was readily apparent in T. W. and Mary Helen Wilson's almost fifty-nine-year marriage. It is a commitment to stay in love, realizing it takes hard work. It is not all fun, nor is it easy, but it is without question worth it. When a couple has been faithfully married for years, it speaks volumes to the world about their faith.

Dr. Nathaniel Branden, a California psychologist, says there are seven keys to a happy marriage:

1. They frequently say, "I love you."
2. They are physically affectionate, holding hands, hugging, cuddling.
3. They express their love sexually.
4. They verbalize their appreciation and admiration.
5. They share their thoughts and feelings, learning to self-disclose what's on their minds and hearts to each other, confiding in each other.
6. They express their love materially, giving little gifts to each other.
7. They create time alone together.[10]

Next-level influencers know that to keep a healthy marriage, they will have to put effort into doing these things.

4. Live to Serve

Next-level influencers do not have an ulterior motive in building a relationship with someone. They seek only to demonstrate to that person the love of Jesus Christ and to serve. Albert Schweitzer said, "Of this I am certain. The only ones among you who will be truly happy are those who have sought and found how to serve."[11] We lose our influence when we attempt to get close to people in order to use them for our advantage.

We see this servant attitude in Jonathan's relationship with David, John the Baptist's relationship with Jesus, and Barnabas's relationship with Paul. The motive is to serve, not be served; to give, not get. As Calvin Coolidge said, "No person was ever honored for what he received. Honor has been the reward for what he gave."[12]

While addressing a graduating class at Southern University in Baton Rouge, Louisiana, Bill Cosby told about a lesson in perspective he learned while studying philosophy in college. The class was debating the age-old question of whether the glass is half empty or half full.

Cosby took the issue home to run it by his father. Without hesitation the elder Cosby said, "It depends on whether you're pouring or drinking." That response helped Cosby earn an A while impressing both his professor and his peers. This simple thought reminds us that things seem worse when we're taking (drinking) and better when we're giving (pouring).[13]

Harry Emerson Fosdick said, "One of the most amazing things ever said on earth is Jesus' statement, 'He that is greatest among you shall be your servant.' None have one chance in a billion of being thought of as really great a century after they're gone, except those who have been servants of all."[14]

We build relationships with people because we care and wish to invest in their well-being. It is never about, "What's in it for me?" One of T. W.'s favorite quotes that Jimmy and Sally grew up hearing was, "Only one life, 'twill soon be past. Only what's done for Christ will last." He was describing next-level influence.

NOTES

Acknowledgments

1. Unless otherwise noted, quotations from these individuals, as well as T. W. Wilson, are from personal interviews with the author.

Chapter 1: What Is Next-Level Influence?

1. Benjamin Franklin, quoted in Paul Lee Tan, *Encyclopedia of 15,000 Illustrations* (Dallas: Bible Communications, 1998), 1253.

2. "Happy Birthday America," sermon by Bruce Howell, Sermon Central, http:// www.sermoncentral.com/sermon.asp?SermonID=37067&ContributorID=4805.

3. W. A. Criswell, *Acts* (Grand Rapids: Zondervan, 1983), 187–88.

4. Mark Sanborn, *The Fred Factor* (New York: Currency, 2004), 3–7.

5. Paul Fritz, www.sermoncentral.com,illustrations,topic:influence.

6. "One Solitary Life" is an essay adapted from the sermon "Arise Sir Knight" in Dr. James Allan Francis, *The Real Jesus and Other Sermons* (Philadelphia: Judson Press, 1926), 123–24.

7. Phillip Schaff, *The Person of Christ* (Garland, TX: American Tract Society, 1913).

8. Information from Billy Graham Center archives, Billy Graham Center, Wheaton College, Wheaton, IL.

9. Dr. Robert Earl Robinson, telephone interview with author, June 3, 2004.

Chapter 2: Who Was T. W. Wilson?

1. William T. Ellis, *Billy Sunday: The Man and His Message* (Chicago: John C. Winston Company, 1936).

Chapter 3: Spiritual Mile Markers

1. Henry T. Blackaby and Claude V. King, *Experiencing God* (Nashville: LifeWay Press, 1990), 15.

2. Quoted in William Martin, *A Prophet with Honor: The Billy Graham Story* (New York: William Morrow and Company, 1991), 205.

3. Ibid., 289.

4. William R. "Bill" Bright Memorial Website, public home page, http://billbright.ccci.org/public.

5. Ronald Reagan, *An American Life* (New York: Simon & Schuster, 1990), 1.

6. George W. Truett, quoted in Robert Morgan, *Nelson's Complete Book of Stories, Illustrations, and Quotes* (Nashville: Thomas Nelson, 2000), 368.

7. W. Glyn Evans, quoted in Roy B. Zuck, *The Speaker's Quote Book* (Grand Rapids: Kregel, 1997), 173.

8. Henrietta C. Mears, quoted in Mary Beth Brown, *Hand of Providence* (Nashville: WND Books, 2004), 192.

9. Dietrich Bonhoeffer, quoted in William Sykes, *The Eternal Vision* (Peabody, MA: Hendrickson, 2002), 362.

10. Charlie "Tremendous" Jones, quoted in Mark Water, comp., *The New Encyclopedia of Christian Quotations* (Grand Rapids: Baker, 2000), 979.

Chapter 4: "Hello, Mr. President"

1. This note is written on Western Springs Baptist Church letterhead and dated November 17, 1943.

2. John Pollock, *Billy Graham, Evangelist to the World* (Minneapolis: World Wide Publications, 1979), 169.

3. Martin, *A Prophet with Honor*, 297.

4. Personal correspondence from George H. W. Bush, May 24, 2001.

5. Personal correspondence, Barbara Bush, May 26, 2001.

6. Personal correspondence, George H. W. Bush, January 2001.

7. Anonymous source, quoted in Water, *New Encyclopedia of Christian Quotations*, 531.

8. Alan C. Emery Jr., "In the Presence of Jesus," *Decision*, July/August 2001, 19.

Chapter 5: Beloved Barnabas

1. Personal correspondence from Johnny Cash, May 2000.

2. Doug Fields, conference speech, Saddleback Community Church, July 20, 1997.

3. Rev. David Holwick, "Two Ounce Slab of Trouble," sermon, June 26, 1994, http://tonga.globat.com/~holwick.com/james/serm94v.txt.

4. Steve Sjogren, *Conspiracy of Kindness* (Ann Arbor, MI: Vine Books, 1993), 18.

5. Robert C. Shannon, *1000 Windows* (Cincinnati: Standard Publishing Company, 1997), 141.

6. Stephen R. Covey, *The 7 Habits of Highly Effective People* (New York: Simon & Schuster, 1989), 31.

7. Victor E. Frankl, quoted in Morgan, *Stories, Illustrations, and Quotes*, 36.

8. Anonymous source, quoted in Water, *New Encyclopedia of Christian Quotations*, 92.

9. Winston Churchill, quoted in Water, *New Encyclopedia of Christian Quotations*, 93.

10. Mark R. Littleton, "The Fine Art of Encouragement," *Reader's Digest*, November 1989, 141–43.

11. Jack Kytle, quoted in Tan, *Encyclopedia of 15,000 Illustrations*, 704–5.

Chapter 6: Close Calls

1. Martin, *A Prophet with Honor*, 545.

2. Ibid., 597.

3. Brown, *Hand of Providence*, 196.

4. John Wesley, quoted in Morgan, *Stories, Illustrations, and Quotes*, 383.

5. Leslie B. Flynn, *Come Alive with Illustrations* (Grand Rapids: Baker, 1987), 142.

6. John Hull and Tim Elmore, *Pivotal Praying* (Nashville: Thomas Nelson, 2002), 4, 11.

7. *Merriam-Webster's Collegiate Dictionary*, 11th ed. (Springfield, MA: Merriam-Webster, 2003).

8. Vance Havner, *Though I Walk Through the Valley* (Old Tappan, NJ: Fleming H. Revell, 1974), 23.

Chapter 7: Counseling Mr. Graham

1. Billy Graham, *Just As I Am: The Autobiography of Billy Graham* (New York: HarperCollins, 1997), 118.

2. Preaching Today Inc., *More Perfect Illustrations for Every Topic* (Wheaton: Tyndale, 2003), 198.

3. Oliver Cromwell, quoted in Water, *New Encyclopedia of Christian Quotations*, 1077.

4. J. I. Packer, *Knowing God* (Downers Grove, IL: InterVarsity, 1973), 80.

5. John C. Maxwell, *The 21 Indispensable Qualities of a Leader* (Nashville: Thomas Nelson, 1999), 44.

6. Lyndon Johnson, quoted in Water, *New Encyclopedia of Christian Quotations*, 281.

7. Flynn, *Come Alive with Illustrations*, 193–94.

8. William Wilberforce, quoted in Morgan, *Stories, Illustrations, and Quotes*, 175.

9. George Sweeting, *Who Said That?* (Chicago: Moody, 1994), 159.

10. Dean Rusk, quoted in R. Daniel Watkins, *An Encyclopedia of Compelling Quotations* (Peabody, MA: Hendrickson, 2001), 436.

11. Raymond McHenry, *McHenry's Stories for the Soul* (Peabody, MA: Hendrickson, 2001), 240.

12. Gigi Graham Tchividjian, "How Do You Find the Time?" *Moody*, November 1991, 72–73.

Chapter 8: Bob Hope, Romans 8:28

1. Betty Frist, *My Neighbors: The Billy Grahams* (Nashville: Broadman Press, 1983), 150–51.

2. Charles M. Schulz, quoted in Glenn Van Ekeren, *Speaker's Sourcebook II* (Englewood Cliffs, NJ: Prentice Hall, 1994), 201.

3. Herbert Gardner, quoted in Water, *New Encyclopedia of Christian Quotations*, 594.

4. Victor Borge, quoted in Water, *New Encyclopedia of Christian Quotations*, 594.

5 Anonymous source, quoted in Van Ekeren, *Speaker's Sourcebook II*, 202.

6. Dwight D. Eisenhower, quoted in Water, *New Encyclopedia of Christian Quotations*, 594.

7. Abraham Lincoln, quoted in Water, *New Encyclopedia of Christian Quotations*, 595.

8. Dr. Michael Miller, quoted in Preaching Today Inc., *More Perfect Illustrations for Every Topic*, 151.

9. Ibid., 152.

Chapter 9: Shhh! Don't Tell

1. *Today in the Word*, Moody Bible Institute, July 1990, 35.

2. Robert C. Shannon, *1000 Windows*, 106.

3. John Calvin, quoted in Water, *New Encyclopedia of Christian Quotations*, 774.

4. *Prevention*, August 1998, 40.

Chapter 10: The Accountability Factor

1. Paul Hoversten, "Brittle Rivets Might Have Doomed the Titanic," *USA Today*, January 28, 1998.

2. McHenry, *McHenry's Stories for the Soul*, 6.

3. More suggested questions by Jim Clayton can be found online at http://www.menofintegrity.org/articles/accountabilityquestions.html.

4. Billy Graham Center Archives Home Page, "What part did the Modesto Manifesto play in the ministry of Billy Graham?" Billy Graham Center at Wheaton College, http://www.wheaton.edu/bgc/archives/faq/4.htm.

5. Truman Brown, quoted in McHenry, *McHenry's Stories for the Soul*, 124.

6. John Beukema, "Fast Food Bill Demands Personal Responsibility," www.preachingtoday.com, topic: accountability, page 6.

7. Lee Eclov, "'Clean-Living Assistants' Provide Accountability," www.preachingtoday.com, topic: accountability, page 5.

Chapter 11: No Room for Wimps

1. Graham, *Just As I Am*, 28.

2. Martin, *A Prophet with Honor*, 461.

3. John McCain, *Why Courage Matters* (New York: Random House, 2004), 9.

4. Ralph Waldo Emerson, quoted in Water, *New Encyclopedia of Christian Quotations*, 232.

5. Robert Kennedy, quoted in "Aldem's Political Quotations: Apt and Otherwise," http://members.tripod.com/aldems/page13.html.

6. John Wesley, quoted in Tan, *Encyclopedia of 15,000 Illustrations*, 451.

7. John Witherspoon, quoted in Watkins, *An Encyclopedia of Compelling Quotations*, 251.

8. Martin Luther, quoted in Sweeting, *Who Said That?*, 125.

9. Morgan, *Stories, Illustrations, and Quotes*, 152–53.

10. Francis Schaeffer, quoted in Water, *New Encyclopedia of Christian Quotations*, 219.

11. Terry Felber, *Am I Making Myself Clear?* (Nashville: Thomas Nelson, 2002), 108–11.

12. McHenry, *McHenry's Stories for the Soul*, 57.

13. Covey, *The 7 Habits of Highly Effective People*, 239–40.

Chapter 12: What Character Looks Like

1. J. H. Bomberger, quoted in Tan, *Encyclopedia of 15,000 Illustrations*, 280.

2. Graham, *Just As I Am*, 37.

3. "T. W. Wilson: The Real Deal," editorial, *Asheville Citizen-Times*, May 27, 2001.

4. McHenry, *McHenry's Stories for the Soul*, 31.

5. John R. W. Stott, quoted in Water, *New Encyclopedia of Christian Quotations*, 162.

6. Larry J. Michael, *Spurgeon on Leadership* (Grand Rapids: Kregel, 2003), 83.

7. Chrysostom, quoted in Zuck, *Speaker's Quote Book*, 201.

8. Shannon, *1000 Windows*, 127.

9. Vance Havner, quoted in Morgan, *Stories, Illustrations, and Quotes*, 461.

10. A. W. Tozer, *The Pursuit of God* (Camp Hill, PA: Christian Publications, 1982), 113.

11. Augustine of Hippo, quoted in Water, *New Encyclopedia of Christian Quotations*, 614.

12. Zuck, *Speaker's Quote Book*, 231.

13. PreachingToday.com Editors, comp., *Perfect Illustrations* (Wheaton: Tyndale, 2002), 160–61.

14. "Billy Graham's Soul Mate: Life Together," *Christianity Today*, July 9, 2001, 26.

15. Theodore Roosevelt, quoted in Water, *New Encyclopedia of Christian Quotations*, 352.

16. Herbert V. Prochrow, "A Businessman's Prayer," quoted in Tan, *Encyclopedia of 15,000 Illustrations*, 279.

Chapter 13: Family and Friends

1. Letter from Billy Graham to T. W. Wilson dated January 19, 1942.

2. Author's personal audio transcript from his presence at the memorial.

3. Ibid.

4. Susan Dryman, "Colleagues Reflect on T. W. Wilson," *Asheville Citizen-Times*, May 29, 2001.

5. Mother Teresa, quoted in Water, *New Encyclopedia of Christian Quotations*, 942.

6. Patrick Morley, Kathy Collard Miller, and D. Larry Miller, comp., *God's Chicken Soup for the Spirit* (Lancaster, PA: Starburst Publishers, 1996), 23.

7. Julian Lennon, quoted in PreachingToday.com Editors, *Perfect Illustrations*, 89.

8. Robert D. Putnam, *Bowling Alone* (New York: Simon & Schuster, 2000), 18–19.

9. Alan Loy McGinnis, *The Power of Optimism* (San Francisco: Harper & Row, 1990), 45.

10. Dr. Nathaniel Branden, quoted in Morgan, *Stories, Illustrations, and Quotes*, 533.

11. Albert Schweitzer, quoted in Water, *New Encyclopedia of Christian Quotations*, 941.

12. Calvin Coolidge, quoted in Water, *New Encyclopedia of Christian Quotations*, 938.

13. McHenry, *McHenry's Stories for the Soul*, 215.

14. Harry Emerson Fosdick, quoted in Quotations Central, Service Quotations, http://www.futurehealth.org/Service_quotations.htm.

Jay Dennis (D.Min., Fuller Theological Seminary) is the pastor of First Baptist Church, Lakeland, Florida, a congregation of over five thousand members. He is a popular conference and seminar speaker and has authored six books, including *Dangerous Intersections* and *The Jesus Habits*. Jay also has a weekly television show, *Strategies4Life*, that is broadcast across the United States, and he uses humor to reach the central Florida area through his daily radio program, *Just a Minute*. He and his wife, Angie, have two children.